First published in 2008 by Jacqui Small LLP

An imprint of Aurum Press Ltd

7 Greenland Street

London NW1 0ND

Publisher Jacqui Small

Commissioning Editor Joanna Copestick

Project Editor Zia Mattocks

Art Director Barbara Zuñiga

Prop Stylist Jo Barnes

Production Peter Colley

ISBN: 978 1 906417 05 5

A catalogue record for this book is available
from the British Library.

2010 2009 2008

10 9 8 7 6 5 4 3 2 1

Printed and bound in Singapore

For Samuel and Nathaniel
And in memory of my dear dad, David Creasey

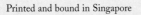

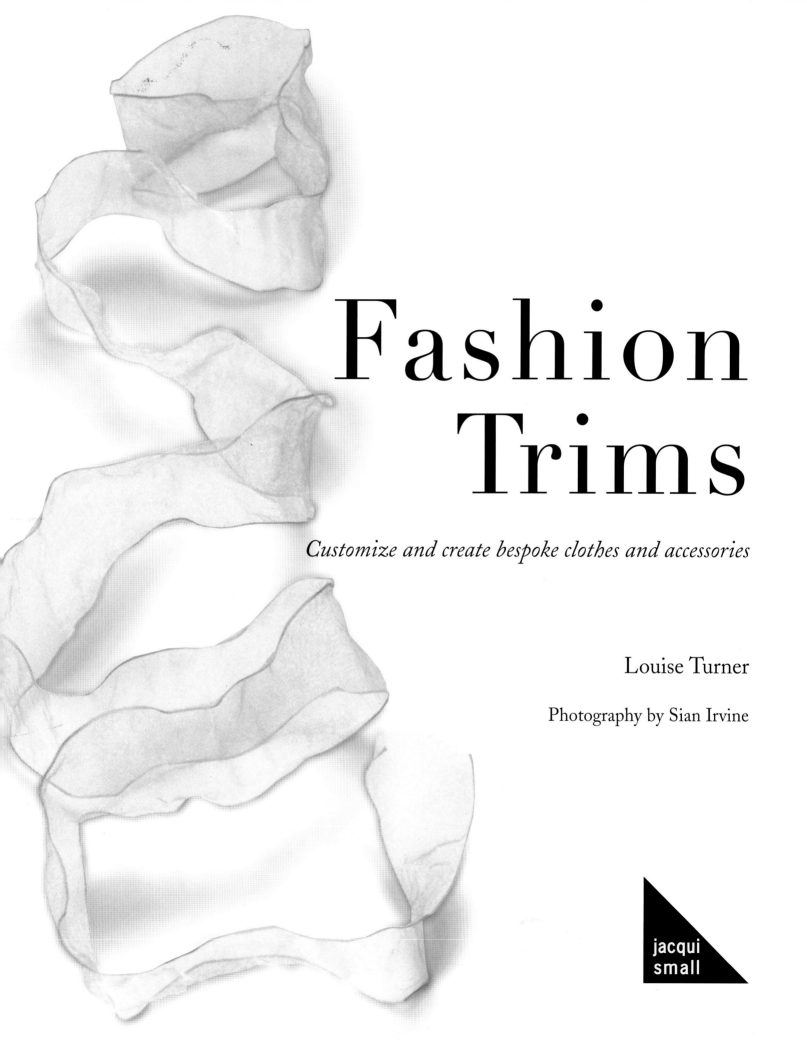

Fashion Trims

Customize and create bespoke clothes and accessories

Louise Turner

Photography by Sian Irvine

jacqui small

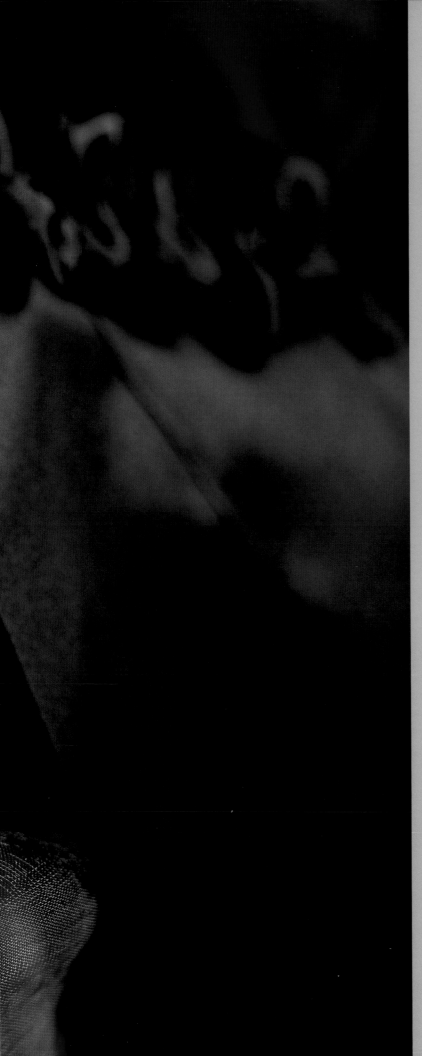

Contents

Introduction

This book will help to solve the eternal dilemma of what to wear and will ensure that your outfit will be unique. When you can't find the perfect dress for a party, buy a plain one and add ruffles of ribbon and a sumptuous sash. If your shoes don't match, decorate them with a Suffolk puff or a ribbon rosette that ties in with the rest of your outfit. When you can't wear something again because everyone's seen it, customize it with some sparkly ribbon trim to give it a new look. Make a pretty bag to go with an outfit or an extravagant hat to match a special get-up. With so many wonderful ribbons and trimmings available, the ideas are limitless.

I've enjoyed sewing since I was a little girl. My mother always made clothes, soft furnishings and other decorative pieces – she is a painter, so she introduced me to colour and design as well as teaching me how to sew. In those days, sewing wasn't just a hobby – cheap clothing was not as readily available as it is today, so if you wanted something special yet affordable, you made it yourself. I made a lot of my own clothes from recycled fabrics – a peplum jacket from a pair of beautiful ruby-red and gold woven brocade curtains, and knickerbockers from a long, luscious midnight-blue velvet evening skirt. I collected vintage clothing made from gorgeous fabrics, such as velvet, satin, lace, crepe, organza and silk. I'd alter and adapt things to wear. I've always loved the extravagance of theatrical costumes, so my clothes often had a certain dramatic element – often eliciting comments of wry amusement from my parents.

Although I've refined my sewing skills over the years, most of the techniques I use in my design work and in this book are actually very straightforward – gathering, pleating, couching, or simply sewing on a length of ribbon and adding some beads. What makes the effect so dramatic and exciting is the design – the choice of colours and the range of ribbon and trims used. Many things inspire my work – the bright, rich colours and textures in a garden full of flowers or the patterns and muted greys and soft yellows found on a beach. Historical costumes also offer a wealth of ideas when it comes to fashion trims. Look back at an era when the addition of ribbons and embellishment with beads, feathers and embroidery was the height of fashion and look at all the fantastic hats, bags and other accessories. Of course, contemporary fashion design is also a rich source of inspiration.

You may want to make items from scratch using new or recycled fabric – you could always use a beautiful piece of vintage fabric to make a clutch bag, for example, such as the one on page 96. Look out for items of clothing that you can cut up to make a bag or scarf: this is a good way to reinvent things that are made of lovely fabric but are damaged or worn in certain places – just cut around those areas. You may have

items of clothing in your wardrobe that you could customize, such as a top you haven't worn for ages or a skirt you are bored with. Or, like the Gold Evening Scarf on page 74, which I couldn't use because its fringe had become so matted, you may have items that can be revamped to give them a new lease of life.

As well as vintage garments that can be reused and adapted, there are many high street stores offering a huge array of affordable clothing. A simple cotton dress can be made into a very special and unique party dress, and a cheap pair of shoes can be transformed into stunning and stylish footwear. Once you start looking around, it's amazing how many things you can find to customize – you'll soon have a whole new wardrobe.

As for trims themselves, there are so many fabulous designs available in every colour and texture imaginable – sparkly, beaded, buttoned, velvet, organza, taffeta, fur, feathers, silk, raffia, patterned, plain, textured, narrow or wide. Take all these permutations into consideration when you are planning a design and the possibilities are endless.

I hope you enjoy making the following projects and that you will be inspired to create more of your own. All you need to get started is a basic sewing kit (see opposite).

Louise

Sewing Kit

Small scissors – a good sharp pair for cutting thread, braid and ribbon.

Dressmaker's cutting-out scissors – a large sharp pair for cutting fabric and wide ribbons. Use these to cut the ends of ribbons diagonally to finish.

Dressmaker's pins – make sure your pins are sharp and smooth. Use them for pinning seams and ribbons in place before sewing. Always try to remove pins just before machine-stitching delicate fabrics, such as organza, silk and satin, as they can tear the fabric if they get caught.

Needles – for hand-sewing. You will need a good selection: very fine ones for threading through little embroidery beads and longer ones for hand-gathering running stitches.

Sewing machine – a sewing machine with straight and zigzag stitch, plus an ordinary presser foot, zip foot and embroidery foot. You will need to change your stitch length to sew machine gathers, but otherwise, for seams and where braid or ribbon is machined on, use a medium-length stitch. Most importantly, when machine-stitching organza, silk or satin, use a sharp, new needle (70 is a suitable size), as a blunt one will damage the fabric.

Threads – always choose a good colour match so that your stitches are less visible; good-quality polyester thread is fine.

Thimble – for pushing a needle through thick layers of fabric or tough materials, such as leather.

Safety pins – for threading ribbon through casings and for temporarily holding ribbon in place, such as when plaiting three ribbons together.

Flexible tape measure – for measuring the length of areas to be decorated with trims, such as around a skirt hem or a cuff, and for measuring lengths of braid or ribbon.

Ruler – for measuring the distances between folds when ribbon is being pleated or when braid is being stitched into a pattern. Also for measuring the placement of trims, such as puffs, ensuring equal distances in between.

Iron and ironing board – to press seams or iron-on interfacing and to press ribbon, either before you use it or once it has been machined on flat. Always make sure you set your iron to the correct temperature and use a cool iron for delicate fabrics. Never iron on the right side of velvet as it will crush the pile.

Ribbons & Trims

There are so many gorgeous ribbons and trims available that we are spoilt for choice. Sometimes it is really difficult to decide which one to choose, but if you buy it because you love it, you will find a use for it. Enjoy experimenting with a length of ribbon to see how it works best. Try folding it or gathering it up in your fingers, be inventive and creative – there are no rules.

Organza, or organdie, comes in a huge range of colours and widths, and as you gather or pleat it, the colour intensifies. Shot organza is amazing and doesn't need much gathering to show off its two-tone effect. Being a sheer or transparent fabric, organza also works well in a single layer to create a delicate coloured edge on a neckline, for example.

Satin ribbon is available in a wide range of colours and widths. Wide pieces are wonderful for making ruffles, as the sheen of the fabric reflects the light and enhances the three-dimensional textures created by gathering or pleating. Use narrower satin ribbons in rows to create stripes and use the tiny 3mm-wide ribbon for ties or laces.

Velvet ribbons in rich, luscious colours are very enticing. Use them to make chokers or belts. Plait double-sided velvet ribbon or use it for ties or handles. Make velvet bows or rosettes for corsages or hats.

Taffeta and wire-edged ribbons come in an exquisite range of colours, shot and multicolours. The wire edging enables you to create very sculptural effects and textures with stiffened ruffles.

Left: A selection of ribbons and trims from V V Rouleaux:
1   Grosgrain STR 19023, colour 5, 15mm.
2   Grosgrain GRO 09099, colour 54, 25mm.
3   Satin ribbon SAT 10125, colour 6838, 25mm.
4   Gingham ribbon GIN 13638, colour 107, 24mm.
5   Pleated organdie PLT 19106, 100mm.
6   Linen jacquard ribbon 17533, colour 557, 40mm.
7   Taffeta ribbon TAF 12384, colour 10, 38mm.
8   Taffeta ribbon TAF 12185, colour 13, 10mm.
9   Taffeta ribbon TAF 12185, colour 15, 10mm.
10 Braid BRD 13713, colour 48, 15mm.
11 Satin ribbon SAT 13783, colour 46, 50mm.
12 Velvet ribbon VEL 10130, colour 9614, 7mm.
13 Fashion trimming BRD 50-6534, colour 2035/59, 20mm.
14 Wire-edged ribbon WIR 08127, colour 233, 40mm.

Grosgrain and linen jacquards often have a lovely natural look – you can use them to trim bags, jackets or hats, while the wider ones are ready-made belts. You can add decorative braids, tapes or gimps to give the belt, or other garments, a wonderful texture that is also rich in colour. Adding gold or silver jacquards or metallic braids immediately creates a special eveningwear look.

Attaching a luxurious textured trim, such as fur or a wide piece of coloured lace, completely changes the look and feel of a garment, transforming it from plain and everyday to unique and rather special.

Cords – narrow or thick, matt or shiny – are great for couching on, either to create single designs, or rows in one colour or a combination.

There are also many trims, such as raffia and bobble fringes in an array of bright colours, that are ideal for decorating baskets or skirt and jacket hems, or anything else you like. Have fun exploring the possibilities of all these different ribbons, braids and trims, but remember that most of them need special cleaning care, so check this with the supplier. Adding trims to a previously machine-washable garment may mean that it has to be dry-cleaned.

Beads

Beads of all shapes, sizes and materials make fantastic decorative additions to sewing projects in so many ways. They can be used to link up colours in designs, to add texture or to bring some sparkle. Large beads can be used instead of buttons or to make a statement – in the middle of a rosette, for instance. They are also useful for hiding stitching – such as in the centre of a Suffolk puff or along a line of machine-stitching, as on the Silver Beaded Neckpiece on page 22 – or for concealing the hems on the ends of ribbons or braids. Small embroidery beads, which are readily available in a wide range of colours from haberdashery stores, can also be used for these purposes. A good source of unusual or vintage beads, such as pearls or pretty faceted glass beads, are old necklaces, especially broken ones, which can be taken apart and the beads reused.

There are also some exquisite beaded trims and fringes available – some are crystal while others are brightly coloured blues and greens or reds, as well as softer shades. Their weight can add a lovely feel to a scarf, or they can be used to trim a bag opening or to create a fringe around the hem of a top.

Left: A selection of vintage glass beads, ranging in size from 15–20mm diameter, and 3mm-diameter embroidery beads.

Right: A selection of ribbons and trims from V V Rouleaux:
1   Flower tape FLO 16136, colour 11, 9mm.
2   Scroll gimp GIM 07018, colour 10, 15mm.
3   Discontinued.
4   Beaded fringe BEA 10659, colour 34, 40mm.
5   Bobble fringe BOB 8836, colour 60, 20mm.
6   Braid BRD 17976, colour 3, 4mm.
7   Scroll gimp GIM 07018, colour 707, 15mm.
8   Braid BRD 18036, colour 10, 15mm.
9   Braid BRD 18035, colour 0, 15mm.
10 Metallic trimming MET 18886, colour gold/black, 20mm.
11 Metallic trimming MET 17366, colour gold/brown, 20mm.
12 Coloured lace LAC 18165, colour 21, 35mm.
13 Coloured lace LAC 10162, colour 23, 85mm.
14 Jacquard ribbon JAC 18421, colour 800, 40mm.
15 Jacquard ribbon JAQ 11502, colour 332, 20mm.
16 Metallic trimming MET 17359 colour gold 12/brown, 20mm.
17 Fur tape FUR 01183, colour 43, 50mm.
18 Braid BRD 09059 colour 75/23, 5mm.

Techniques

Here are a few basic techniques that I use. Try each one with several types and sizes of ribbon and see the different effects and textures you can create. You can use these techniques in all sorts of ways – for example, you could make small Suffolk puffs out of ribbon and sew them around a hat or the top of a bag; you could make small flowers to put on a basket or use as a corsage; or try decorating a bag with one large bow or trimming the hem of a skirt with rows of ruched ribbon. Practise tying bows and making flowers with an old piece of ribbon. The other techniques are really very simple – it is amazing how a few running stitches can transform a length of ribbon.

Tying a bow

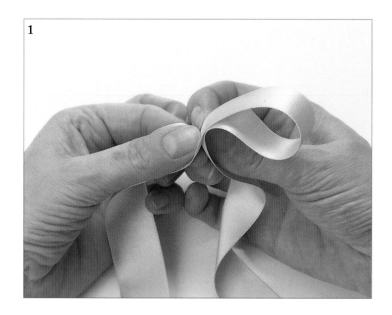

1 Take a 70cm length of ribbon and fold it in half. Holding the centre point, make one side of the ribbon into a loop 9cm long.

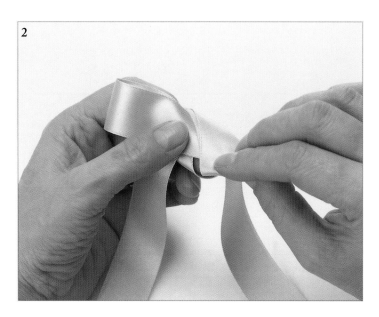

2 Change hands and make the other half of the ribbon into a loop the same size. Keep a finger through the centre and put one loop in front of the other, then bring the loop at the back over to the front.

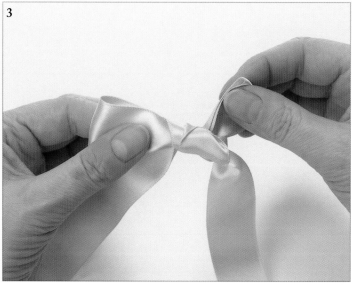

3 Push that loop through the centre where your finger is and begin pulling it through.

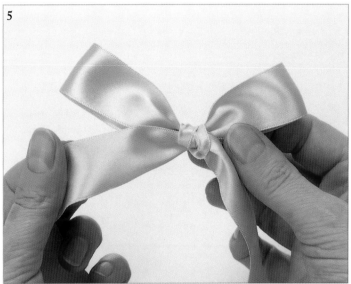

4 Before you tighten the bow, bring the opposite ribbon end over the top and to the front of the central knot.

5 Carefully tighten up the bow and make sure both loops are the same length. To finish, lay the bow down flat and trim the ends diagonally so they are the same length, then paint the ends with clear nail varnish to prevent them from fraying.

Ruched ribbon

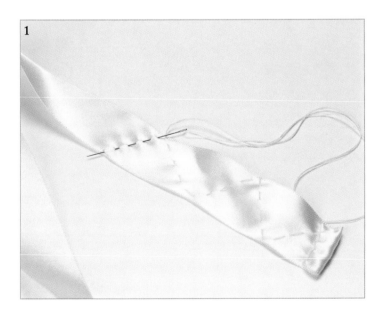

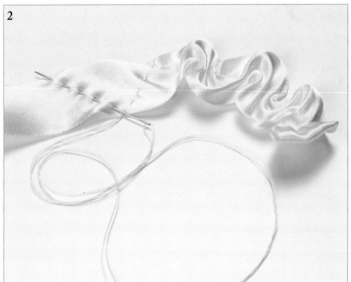

1 Cut a length of ribbon and fold one end under by 5mm. Thread a needle with double thread and knot the ends. Sew this hem down with a line of running stitches. Work a backstitch, then sew a line of running stitches in a zigzag pattern along the length of the ribbon.

2 Gather up the ribbon as you go. When you reach the end, turn under 5mm and finish off with a backstitch to secure the gathers and sew down the hem.

Ribbon rose

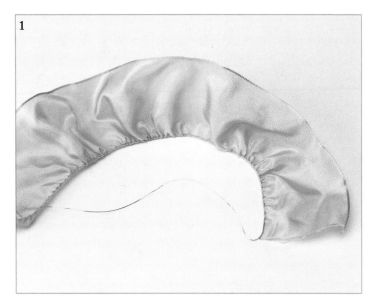

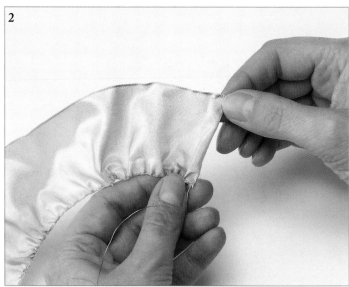

1 Pull the bottom wire at both ends of a length of wire-edged ribbon to gather the fabric slightly.

2 Turn one raw end of the ribbon under twice.

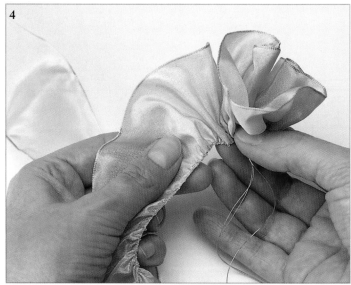

3 Begin to roll up the ribbon, pleating it as you do so. This forms the core of your rose.

4 Thread a needle and secure the thread to the base of the rose with a few stitches.

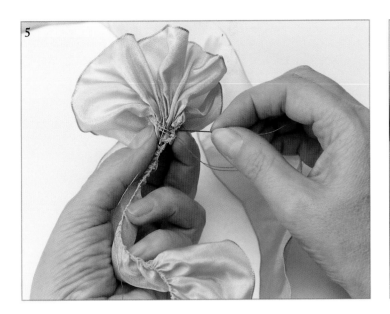

5 Continue rolling up the gathered ribbon, using the needle and thread to catch several pleats in place every so often as you build up the petal effect.

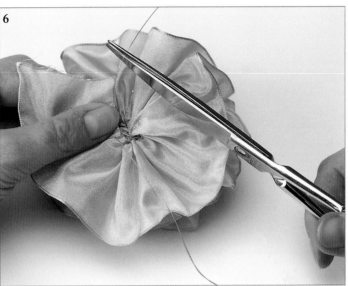

6 When you reach the end of the ribbon, turn the raw ends under. Tie the wire ends together and trim.

7 Secure the base of the rose with a few neat stitches through it. Use this thread to attach the rose to your chosen item.

8 Manipulate the petals with your fingers until you are happy with the finished shape of the rose.

Ribbon rosette

1

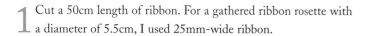

2

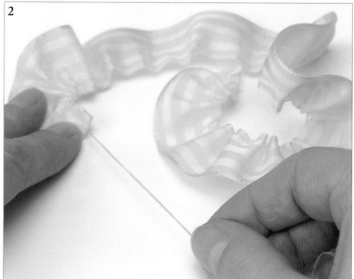

1 Cut a 50cm length of ribbon. For a gathered ribbon rosette with a diameter of 5.5cm, I used 25mm-wide ribbon.

2 Thread a needle with double thread and knot the ends. Turn under 5mm at one end of the ribbon and secure with several backstitches. Then, using running stitch, sew along the bottom edge of the ribbon, gathering up the fabric as you go.

3

4

3 When you have sewn to the other end of the ribbon, turn the raw end under and finish by pulling up your stitches tightly to gather the ribbon into a rosette. Secure the stitching firmly with several backstitches.

4 Sew the ends of the ribbon together. Don't cut the thread, but use it to stitch the rosette in place and sew a bead or button into the centre to finish it.

Suffolk puff

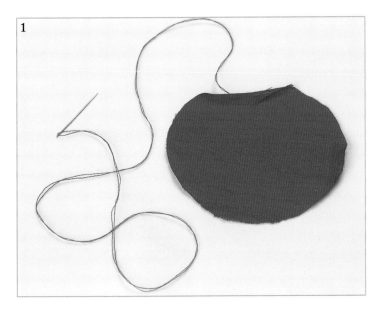

1 For a Suffolk puff with a diameter of 3.5cm, cut a circle of fabric 8cm in diameter (a glass or cup makes a useful pattern to draw around). Thread a needle with double thread and knot the ends. Fold the edge of the fabric over by 4mm and start with a backstitch to secure the thread.

2 Folding the edge over by 4mm as you go, sew a line of running stitches all the way around the circle. Finish with your needle and thread on the inside of the circle.

3 Pull the thread to gather the stitches up as closely as they will go – you may need to manipulate the puff into shape. Secure the puff with several stitches through the centre.

4 Using the same thread, attach the Suffolk puff to your chosen item and sew a bead into the centre to hide the stitches.

Jewellery & Accessories

Silver Beaded Neckpiece

The crystal beaded trim I have used for this sparkling neckpiece is jewel-like in the way it hangs from the silver metallic woven braid. The combination of trims creates a regal accessory that is stunning worn with a simple dress. If you wish, you could just use crystals at the front of the neckpiece and sew other beads to the rest of the braid.

You will need

Silver braid 26mm wide – sufficient to encircle your neck plus 5cm

White buttonhole elastic – sufficient to loop around the button or bead plus 3cm

Crystal beaded trim with 6cm drop – length as above

Crystal beads – approximately 2mm diameter

Crystal button or glass bead – 1.5–2cm diameter

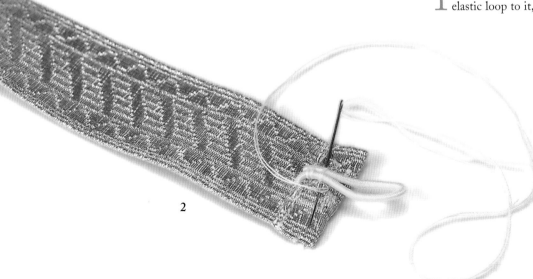

1 Turn one end of the braid under by 5mm and machine-stitch the elastic loop to it, going over it several times so it is very secure.

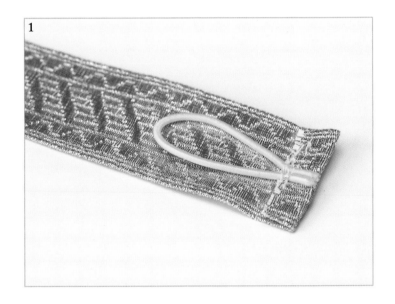

2 Turn the hem over again by 1cm and machine-stitch in place. Use the thread ends from your seam to hand-sew the elastic down so it points in the other direction and the loop overlaps the end of the braid.

Hem the other end of the braid, turning under 5mm and then 1cm and machine-stitching into place.

Work out where you will need to position your button on this end of the neckpiece by wrapping the braid around your neck with the elastic buttonhole on top. Mark this position with a small hand-stitch.

3 With the braid wrong side up and the buttonhole to the right, place the crystal trim right side up on the braid. Turn the end under and ensure the first crystal tassel is in line with the end of the braid. Tack the trim to the braid, making sure that none of the tape shows beneath the bottom edge of the braid on the right side. The last crystal tassel should line up with the stitch marking your button placement. Use the zip foot on your machine to stitch the crystal trim onto the braid along the bottom edge, then remove the tacking.

4 Sew a row of matching crystal beads on the outside of the braid to help hide the line of machine-stitching and to unify the braid and beaded trim. Lastly, sew on the button at the marked position.

Ruby-red Choker

This striking choker has a three-dimensional quality inspired by Elizabethan ruffs. The rich red velvet makes a sumptuous base for the shimmering box-pleated organza that is sewn on top. The pleats have been opened out and held in place by small beads and stitches, making a statement piece that is as striking as any necklace.

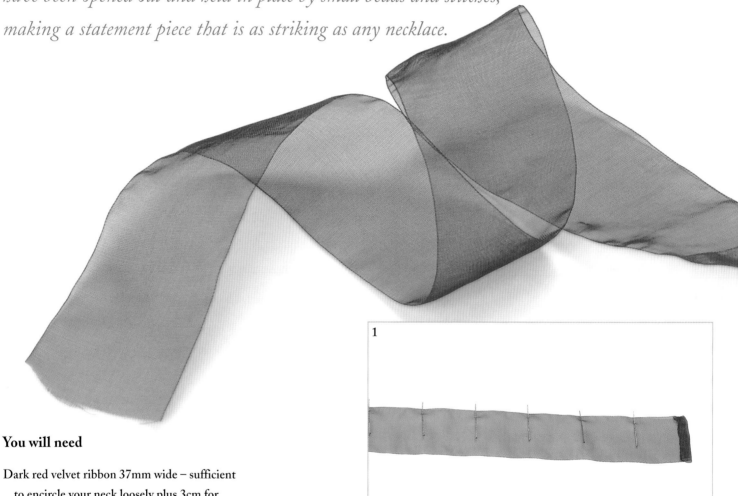

You will need

Dark red velvet ribbon 37mm wide – sufficient to encircle your neck loosely plus 3cm for the hem

Red organza ribbon 40mm wide – three times your neck measurement plus 3cm for hems

Dark red velvet ribbon 4mm wide – the same length as the wide velvet

Hook-and-eye fastening

Selection of matching beads – approximately 2mm diameter

1 Begin by hemming the wide velvet and organza ribbons by folding the ends under, first by 5mm then by 1cm. Hand-sew the hems in place. Check the fit by wrapping the red velvet ribbon around your neck – it should fit snugly, but not too tightly, without overlapping.

To prepare the organza ribbon for box-pleating, lay it horizontally on your work surface, right side up, and put a pin 4cm in from the right-hand end. Add another five pins, one every 4cm.

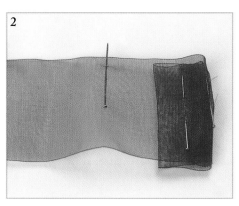

2 Fold the ribbon to the right, so that the first pin is in line with the hemmed edge. Use the marker pin to pin this pleat in place.

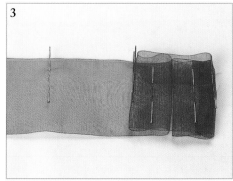

3 Now fold the ribbon to the left at the second pin, bringing it into line with the third pin. Use the marker pin to pin the pleat in place.

Continue pleating by folding the ribbon to the right at the fourth pin, bringing it into line with the third pin, and pin in place. Fold the ribbon to the left at the fifth pin, bringing it into line with the sixth pin, and pin.

Repeat this pattern of pleating along the organza, adding more sets of six pins and folding as above until you reach the end of the ribbon.

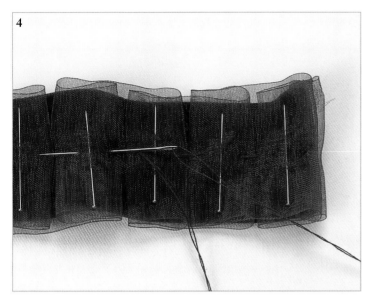

4 Make sure the pleated organza fits exactly over the length of wide velvet ribbon. You may need to adjust some of the pleats to make it the correct length. Use double thread to hand-sew the pleated organza to the velvet ribbon, sewing running stitch through the centre of the ribbons. Make sure you align the edges as you go, as the velvet will make it slippery. Remove the pins as you sew.

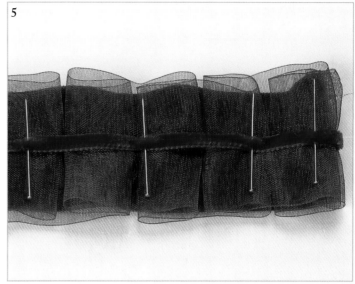

5 Pin the narrow velvet ribbon over the top of your hand-stitches, leaving 1cm overhanging at each end. Turn these ends under and hand-sew them into place on the wrong side. Machine-stitch along the centre of the narrow velvet ribbon.

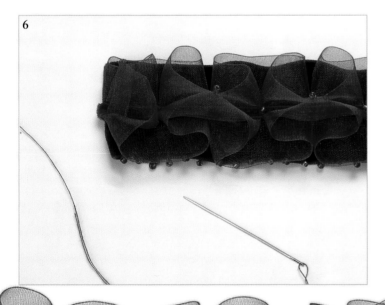

6 Sew a bead onto the narrow velvet ribbon where the folds of the pleats meet. Sew a bead to hold the top and bottom parts of the pleats together to create a more three-dimensional effect. Use a small knot to hold the bead in place. Sew a row of beads along the bottom edge of the wide velvet ribbon.

Sew the hook-and-eye fastening in place at either end of the choker on the back.

Ribbon Rosette Corsage

This is a celebration of two gorgeous wide taffeta ribbons, one plain and one striped in deep autumnal colours. The corsage is made up of one rosette on top of the other, with matching ribbons and beads spilling out of the centre. This corsage complements a tweed jacket or winter coat, but you can make it in any colour to match your outfit.

You will need

Plum, lilac and gold striped wire-edged taffeta ribbon 38mm wide – 50cm

Plum wire-edged taffeta ribbon 50mm wide – 50cm

Plum velvet ribbon 16mm wide – 15cm

Plum velvet ribbon 5mm wide – 15cm

Red organza ribbon 11mm wide – 15cm

Purple organza ribbon 11mm wide – 15cm

42 purple embroidery beads – 2mm diameter

11 gold embroidery beads – 2mm diameter

Clear nail varnish

Sew-on brooch back

1 Make two ribbon rosettes with the striped and plain wire-edged taffeta ribbons, starting with the narrower striped piece (see also page 18). Remove the wire from the bottom edge of the ribbon by pulling it through from one end. Using a double thread knotted at the ends, turn the raw end under. Starting with a backstitch, sew a row of running stitches along the bottom edge of the ribbon. When you reach the end, turn it under and gather up the ribbon into a circle. Leave a small hole in the centre, large enough to insert the tip of your finger. Work a backstitch to secure the gathers. Sew the two ends together on the wrong side. Make the second rosette in the same way, using the wider plain ribbon.

2 Place the small rosette on top of the large one, lining up the seams. Sew the rosettes together with four equally spaced stitches close to the centre. Now sew four more stitches, but this time thread three purple and two gold embroidery beads onto each stitch to create clusters of beads. Finish the thread off securely on the back of the rosette.

3 Take the four 15cm lengths of ribbon and cut one end of each diagonally. Paint this end with clear nail varnish to prevent it from fraying. Place the ribbons one on top of the other with the organza ones on top. Thread the unfinished ends through the centre of the rosettes from front to back, positioning them so they fall over the seams on the rosettes.

4 Using double thread, sew the ends of the ribbons – about 2cm – to the back of the large rosette. Bring the needle and thread to the front for the next step.

5 For the bead stamen, thread ten purple beads onto your thread then one gold bead. Take the thread back through the coloured beads but not through the gold one. Sew right through to the back of the corsage and sew two stitches into the ribbon to secure the beads. Bring the needle and thread to the front of the corsage again. Make two more stamen in the same way.

Sew the brooch back securely onto the back of the large rosette, making sure it is parallel with the bottom of the corsage.

Summer Haircomb

Inspired by the pretty looped fringe, this decorated haircomb, which matches the basket on page 88, is a charming way to put some bright summer colours in your hair. It's the ideal accessory for the beach or poolside and the ribbon rosettes, in luscious striped lemon taffeta, are like mouthwatering citrus slices in an ice-cold drink.

You will need

Haircomb

Orange looped gingham fringe 5.4cm deep –
   2cm longer than the width of the haircomb

Yellow striped ribbon 25mm wide – 1.5m

Three orange beads – 5mm diameter

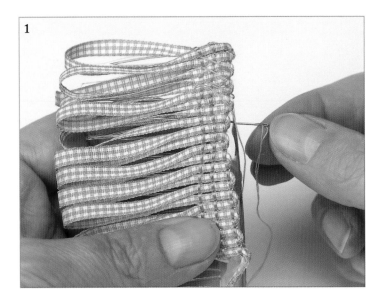

1 Position the gingham fringe on the haircomb with the loops covering the teeth of the comb and 1cm overlapping at each end. Use double thread to sew the fringe in place, starting at one end and turning the hem allowance under. Work along the comb, passing the thread between the teeth and catching the gingham at the top.

2 Cut the yellow striped ribbon into 50cm lengths and make three ribbon rosettes, following the instructions on page 18. Sew the rosettes onto the gingham at the top of the haircomb with an orange bead in the centre of each.

Braided Belt

This belt is made from a length of wide linen tape that is already embroidered along the edges. The braids I've used tie in colourwise and create interesting textures placed close together. You can make a belt like this to go with any item of clothing (see the pencil skirt with matching braided hem on page 122).

You will need

Linen tape with embroidered edge 80mm
   wide – 1.2m

Turquoise braid 15mm wide – 1.2m

Blue flower braid 9mm wide – 2.4m

Green knot braid 9mm wide – 2.4m

Cream braid with turquoise stitch
   5mm wide – 3m

Belt buckle with the prong removed –
   the same width as the tape

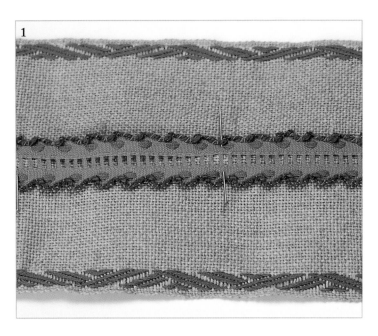

1 Pin the turquoise braid down the centre of the linen tape and machine-stitch it in place along the top and bottom edges.

2 Pin and then machine-stitch a row of blue flower braid along both edges of the linen tape, just inside the embroidery. Press lightly on the wrong side.

Now pin on two rows of green knot braid, positioning one on either side of the central turquoise braid, just above and below the blue flower braid. Hand-sew these in place using a double thread and running stitch, making tiny stitches on the top in the knots of the braid and longer ones on the wrong side of the linen tape.

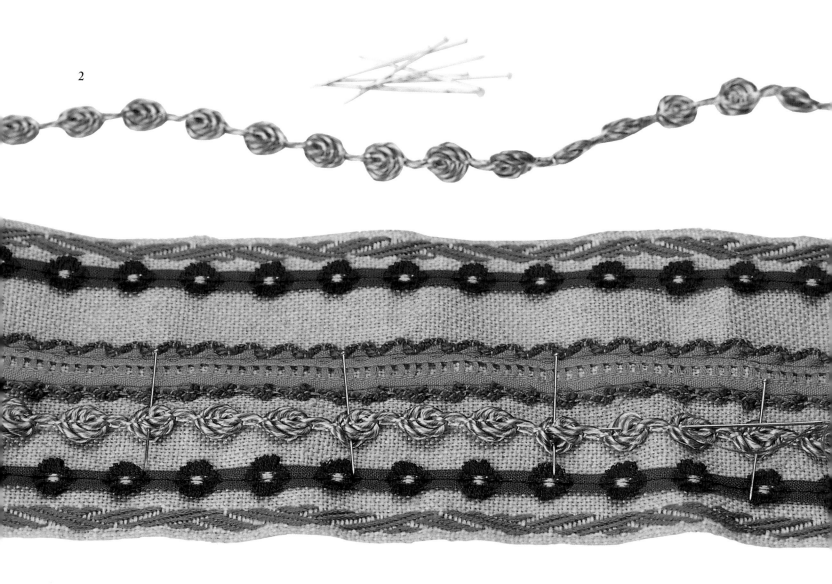

3 Decorate the belt buckle by winding the cream braid around it. Do this by rolling the ribbon into a ball to prevent it from getting tangled and keep passing it through the centre of the buckle, making sure it butts up to itself and leaves no gaps. When you reach the end, turn the raw end under and hand-sew firmly in place.

4 Hem the ends of the braided linen tape, folding the ends over twice and hand-sewing the hem with herringbone stitch to help flatten it. Sew the side sections of the hem together. Fold one end over the centre of the buckle and secure with herringbone stitch.

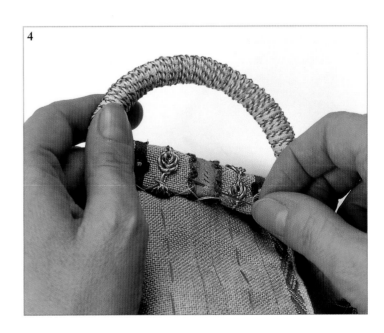

White Fur Gloves

*These elegant and romantic gloves are true 'winter wonderland'
accessories. The combination of the luxurious fur trim, the woven
braid and the glint of crystal beads is reminiscent of the costumes in
a classic Russian love story. Wear them with the matching scarf on
page 82 for the full Dr Zhivago effect – lovely on a snowy day.*

You will need

Pair of white wool gloves

White fur trim 75mm wide – a length twice
the circumference of the widest part of
your hand

White braid 15mm wide – two lengths to
stitch across the front of your gloves plus
6cm for hems

Six crystal beads – 4mm diameter

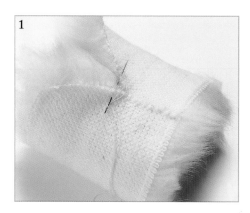

1 Measure the circumference of your hand
at its widest part and cut two pieces of
fur trim to this length. Fold the first piece
in half with right sides together and join it
end to end to form a cuff, tucking all the fur
fibres inside as you hand-sew it together.

2 Turn the fur cuff right side out and
insert the wrist of the glove, making sure
the seam of the cuff is on the palm side of the
glove. Align the edges and hand-sew the cuff
to the glove. You may need to stretch the
glove a little to make it fit. Then sew several
stitches at the bottom of the trim where the
seam meets the glove to hold the fur in place.

3 Hand-sew a strip of braid across the
front of the glove, just below the fur trim,
turning the ends under by 1.5cm. Catch the
edge of the fur trim down with some small
stitches just above the centre of the braid.
Sew three beads onto the front of the glove.
Repeat for the other glove.

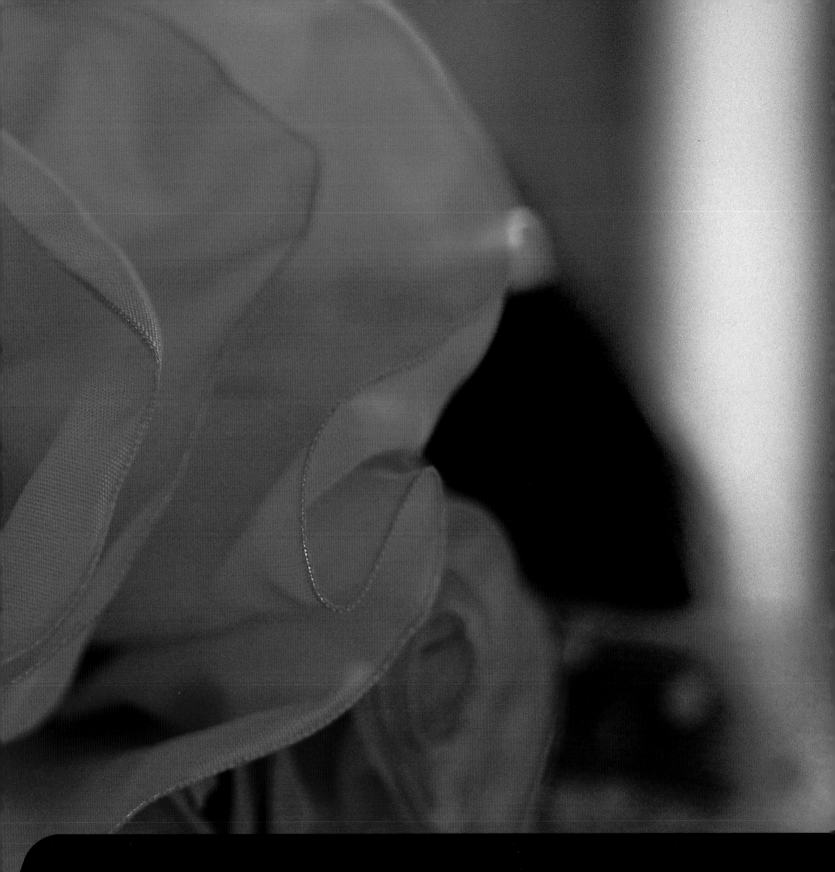

Hats & Shoes

Summer Occasion Hat

This pretty blue hat was unadorned when I found it, but you may find one with decoration on that you can remove. When ribbon is as lovely as this organza, you really need to show it off by letting it hang down in long lengths from the back of the hat. You can make one large flower, as I have, several smaller ones or a mixture of both.

You will need

Lightweight wide-brimmed pale blue hat

Silvery blue satin fabric – 30 x 80cm

Blue/gold shot organza ribbon 105mm
  wide – 2m

Silver organza ribbon 36mm wide – 2m

Dark blue organza ribbon 36mm wide – 2m

Duck-egg blue wire-edged taffeta ribbon
  48mm wide – 1.5m

Clear nail varnish

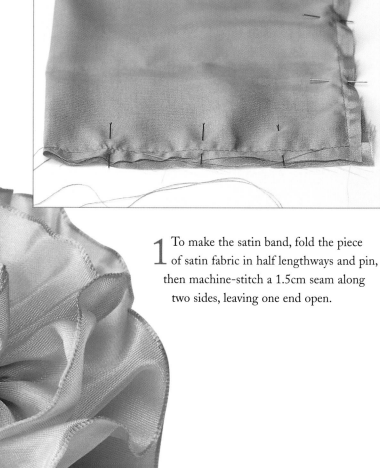

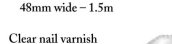

1 To make the satin band, fold the piece of satin fabric in half lengthways and pin, then machine-stitch a 1.5cm seam along two sides, leaving one end open.

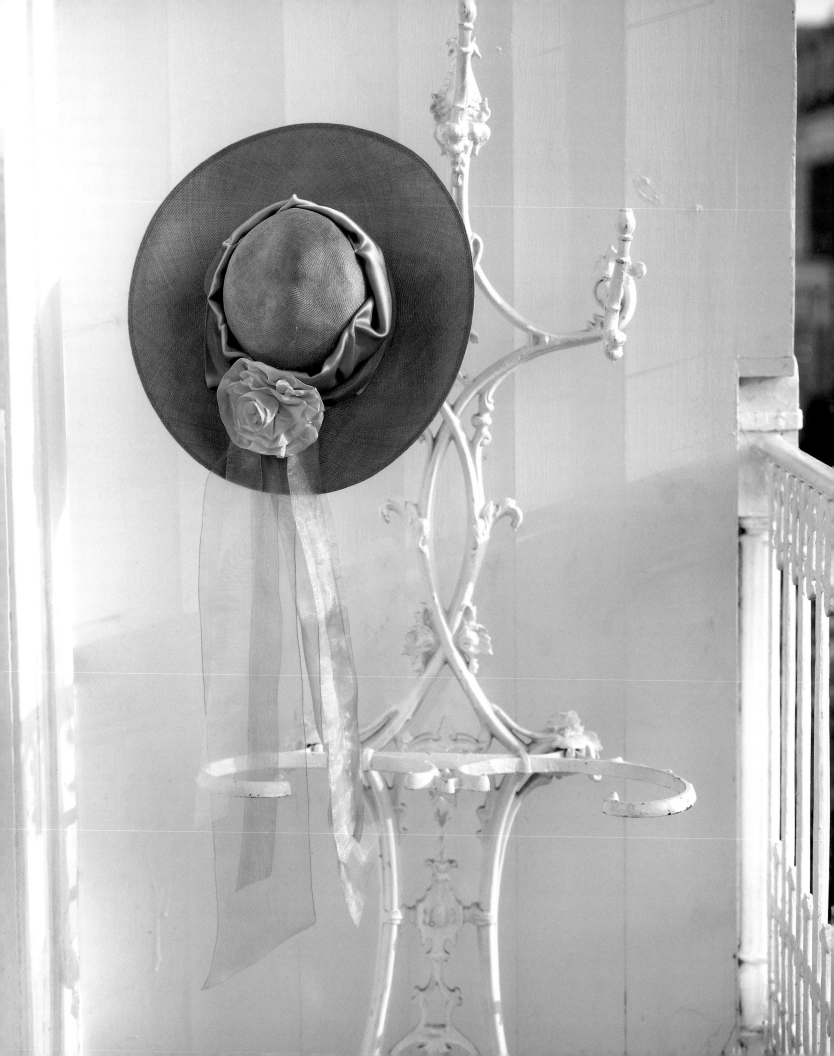

2 Turn the satin band right side out and press. Turn the raw ends under by 5mm and machine-stitch in place.

3 Fold the length of satin over so that the pressed edge is about a quarter of the way down on the inside, and wrap it around the hat. Start at the centre back and tuck the machine-finished end underneath the other end. Pin the satin to the hat in about six places, letting it fall into folds.

4 Sew the band in place at each pin, making a tiny stitch on the outside and trying to hide it under a fold in the satin. Secure the thread ends together on the inside of the hat by tying them in a knot.

5 Cut the ends of all the organza ribbons diagonally and paint them with clear nail varnish to prevent them from fraying. Put the narrow ribbons on top of the wide one.

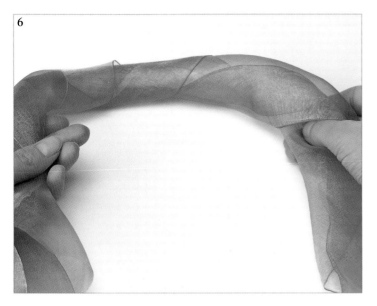

6 Hold the ribbons securely in one hand about 20cm from the centre and twist them together lightly several times. The twisted section of ribbons should be long enough to wrap around the hat.

7 Holding both ends of the twisted section, wrap the ribbons around the hat and knot them together at the back.

8 Follow the instructions on pages 16–17 to make a large rose using the length of wire-edged taffeta ribbon.

Sew the rose securely to the back of the hat, catching the knot of organza ribbons in place at the same time.

Fascinator

*As its name suggests, this project is about creating something
fascinating to wear on your head, so you can really go to town with
feathers, nets and ribbons, and add other decorations such as wax
flowers or beads. Less cumbersome than a hat, a fascinator is great
for a wedding or a day at the races; keep it in place with hair grips.*

You will need

Black fascinator base

Two pieces of spotted net – 50 x 20cm and
   10 x 20cm

Pink/red shot wire-edged taffeta ribbon
   70mm wide – 1m

Red wire-edged taffeta ribbon 35mm
   wide – 1m

Three green feathers

Red feather fan

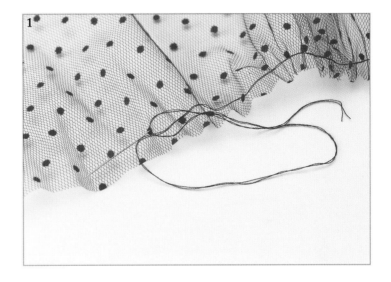

1 Hand-sew a line of running stitches along one long side of the
larger piece of net and gather it up.

2 Sew the gathered edge of the net to the underside of the
fascinator base, keeping the stitches small on top.

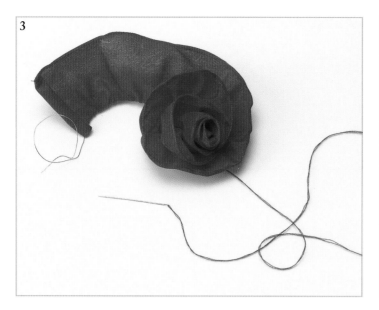

3 Following the instructions on pages 16–17, make a large rose using the 70mm-wide wire-edged taffeta ribbon. Sew a thread onto the underside of the rose and use it to catch the pleats in place every so often as you assemble it.

4 Use the same thread at the base of the rose to sew it onto the centre of the fascinator base.

5 Sew three green feathers onto the front of the fascinator base.

6 Cut the 35mm-wide wire-edged taffeta ribbon in half and make two small roses in the same way as before. Sew these onto the base of the fascinator, using them to hide the ends of the green feathers.

7 Sew the red fan of feathers to the back of the large rose, just catching it in several places with a small discreet stitch.

8 Sew a line of running stitches along one long side of the smaller piece of net, as before, and gather it up. Sew the gathered net to the back of the feather fan to hide its base and support the feathers.

Tie-up Pumps

Inspired by the pretty pink ballet shoes I had as a little girl, these simple pumps were customized with ribbon ties and bow rosettes to go with the summer dress on page 110 – an easy way to match your shoes to any outfit. The bow rosettes are very versatile and could also be used to decorate other clothes and accessories.

You will need

White pumps

Pink satin or silk ribbon 15mm wide – 2.6m

Pink/yellow wire-edged taffeta ribbon 24mm wide – 1.6m

Two glass beads – 1–1.5cm diameter

Clear nail varnish

1 Try your shoes on and mark the point on the inside edge that aligns with the front of your ankle on both sides of the shoe.

Cut four lengths of pink satin ribbon, 65cm long. Sew each piece of ribbon to the inside of the shoe where you have marked, turning the raw ends under by 5mm.

Cut the ends of the ribbon diagonally and paint them with clear nail varnish to prevent them from fraying.

2

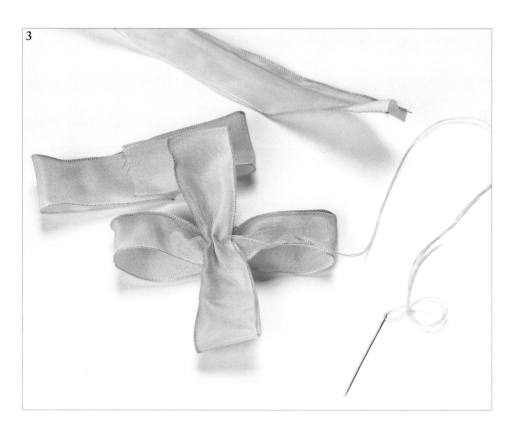

3

2 For each bow rosette, cut four lengths of wire-edged taffeta ribbon, 20cm long. Take the first piece and fold it so that the raw ends overlap in the centre. Thread a needle with a double thread and knot the ends. Stitch into the back of the bow in the centre and sew some running stitches across it, joining the ends of the ribbon together where they overlap. Pull the thread gently to gather the bow in the centre. Don't cut the thread.

3 Fold the second piece of ribbon in the same way and pin it on top of the first to form a cross. Using the same thread, sew the ribbon in place and gather the centre of the second bow as before.

4 Fold the third ribbon and place it diagonally on the second, then sew and gather the centre of the bow as before. Repeat with the fourth piece, placing it on the other diagonal and sewing it in position while gathering the centre of the bow.

Turn the bow rosette over and sew it securely onto the front of the shoe, using a thimble on the third finger of your sewing hand to help push the needle through the leather.

5 Using the same thread, sew a single glass bead into the centre of the bow rosette.

Buckle & Bow Shoes

Buckles and bows have always been used to decorate and fasten shoes and this is a great way to turn plain court shoes into something unique and special. It's also a way to cover up the creases that form in the leather on the front of a shoe. You will need to find a belt buckle – either new or vintage – that's made up of two matching halves.

You will need

Brown court shoes

Brown satin ribbon 50mm wide – 1m

Red/green wire-edged taffeta ribbon 70mm wide – 20cm

Clear nail varnish

Vintage belt buckle formed of two matching halves

1 Use a double thread and a strong, sharp needle to sew the buckle to the front of the shoe, leaving enough space above it to attach the ribbon bow. Wear a thimble on the third finger of your sewing hand to help push the needle through the leather. Start from the inside and leave about 10cm of thread loose for knotting. Sew the buckle on with four stitches at each end and then knot the threads together on the inside of the shoe to secure them.

2 To make each bow, cut a 30cm length of brown satin ribbon and machine-stitch the ends together. Turn the raw ends to the inside and move the seam to the centre of the loop.

For the centre of the bow, cut a 10cm length of wire-edged taffeta ribbon and machine-stitch the ends together, leaving long threads at each end. Turn the raw ends to the inside.

3 Thread the large satin loop through the small taffeta one, keeping the seam on the taffeta at the back and the seam on the satin in the centre.

4 Cut a 20cm length of brown satin ribbon and thread it through the back (seam side) of the taffeta loop behind the satin loop.

Gather up the taffeta loop slightly and sew it in place using the long threads at the end of the seam.

Manipulate the satin pieces to look like a well-balanced bow and use small stitches on the back to catch it in place. Try the bow on the shoe and manipulate and sew it further until it looks right.

Using a thimble, sew the bow securely to the shoe, positioning it just above the buckle and sewing into the back of the bow. As with the buckle, knot the thread ends together inside the shoe.

Finally, cut the ends of the ribbon diagonally, making sure they don't touch the ground, and paint the ends with clear nail varnish to prevent them from fraying.

Hats & Shoes   **59**

Red Espadrilles

This is a simple but effective way to personalize plain espadrilles. I chose red grosgrain tape with small white spots and red organza ribbon with larger white spots to complement my red shoes and create a play on textures. The organza looks very different when it has been gathered up into the rosettes with a vintage pearl bead stitched into the centre for a touch of glamour.

You will need

Red canvas espadrilles

Red and white spotted grosgrain tape 15mm
   wide – 3m

Red and white spotted organza ribbon
   40mm wide – 1m

Two pearl beads or buttons – 1cm diameter

1 To make the ties, cut two 1.5m lengths of spotted grosgrain tape. Turn both ends of each tape over twice by 5mm and hand-sew the hems into place. Remove the old ties from the espadrilles and rethread them with the new ones.

1

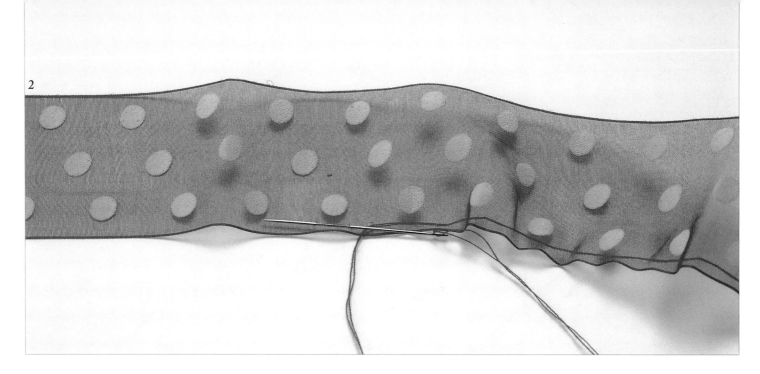

2 Referring also to the instructions on page 18, make two ribbon rosettes using the spotted organza. To do this, first cut a 50cm length of ribbon for each rosette. Thread a needle with a double thread and knot the ends. Turn under 5mm at one end of the ribbon and secure the thread with a backstitch. Using running stitch, sew along the bottom edge of the ribbon, gathering it up as you go.

3 When you reach the end of the ribbon, turn the raw end under and finish pulling up your stitches to gather the ribbon into a rosette. Secure firmly with several backstitches. Oversew the ends together on the back of the rosette.

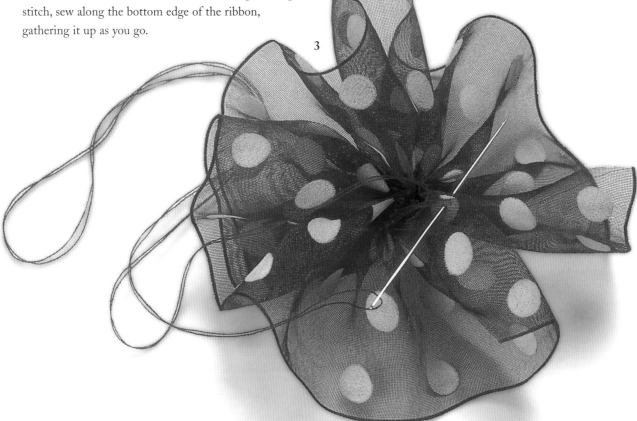

4 Sew a rosette firmly onto the front of each shoe, ensuring that the join on the rosette sits over the canvas part of the shoe.
Sew the pearl into the centre of the rosette and finish the thread off securely on the inside of the shoe.

4

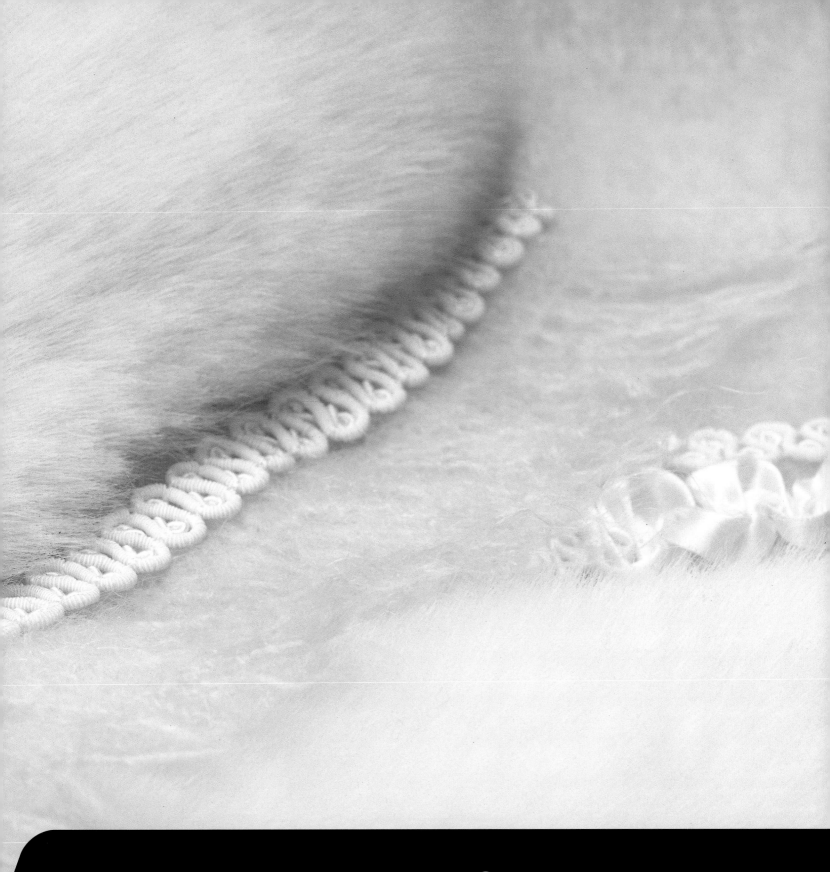

Scarves & Shawls

Pink Taffeta Stole

I found this stole in a second-hand shop. Although plain, it was made of beautiful fabric that I thought would go well with the dress on page 110, so I trimmed it to match. The beaded fringe gives it weight and the ruched yellow organza creates texture against the pink taffeta. Add another row of ruched or plain ribbon and more beads, if you wish.

You will need

Pink taffeta stole – 160 x 44cm

Yellow organza ribbon 21mm wide – twice the length of the stole plus 6cm for hems

Yellow beaded fringe with 5cm drop – a length twice the width of the stole

Pink/yellow taffeta ribbon – a length twice the width of the stole plus 6cm for hems

Yellow and pearl embroidery beads – 2mm diameter

Yellow organza ribbon 40mm wide – a length six times the width of the stole

1 Cut two pieces of 21mm-wide yellow organza ribbon to the same length of the stole plus 3cm for hems. With a 1.5cm hem allowance at each end, pin one length of organza to both long edges of the stole, letting it overhang the edge by 3mm. Turn the raw ends under by 5mm and fold them to the back of the stole. Machine-stitch in place along both edges of the ribbon.

2 Cut two lengths of beaded fringe to the same width as the stole.
Pin the tape of the beaded fringe to the wrong side of the shawl,
making sure the tape doesn't show on the right side. Sew it in place
with two lines of machine-stitching. Oversew the raw ends of the
tape by hand to prevent them from fraying.

3 Cut two lengths of taffeta ribbon to the
same width as the stole plus 3cm for
hems. If the ribbon is wire-edged, remove
the wires by pulling them through. Fold the
raw ends under by 1.5cm and machine-stitch
the ribbon to the right side of the stole, 5mm
from the edge, sewing along both edges of
the ribbon. Make sure you cover the top row
of machine-stitching where you have sewn
on the beaded tape.

Sew a row of matching embroidery beads
along the edges of the shawl below the
taffeta ribbon, spacing them 1cm apart.

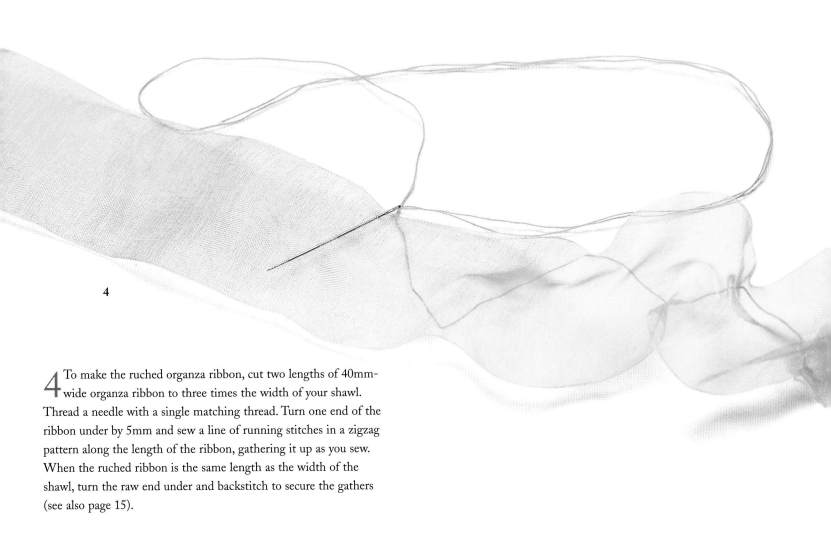

4 To make the ruched organza ribbon, cut two lengths of 40mm-wide organza ribbon to three times the width of your shawl. Thread a needle with a single matching thread. Turn one end of the ribbon under by 5mm and sew a line of running stitches in a zigzag pattern along the length of the ribbon, gathering it up as you sew. When the ruched ribbon is the same length as the width of the shawl, turn the raw end under and backstitch to secure the gathers (see also page 15).

5 Pin the ruched ribbon to the right side of the stole, placing it just above the taffeta ribbon. Machine-stitch it in place down the centre of the ribbon and then remove the hand-sewn gathers.

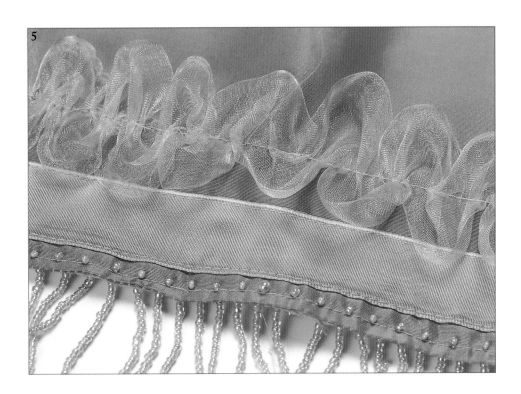

Gathered-ribbon Scarf

This gorgeous, luxurious effect is achieved by gathering several lengths of satin, organza and taffeta ribbon individually and then sewing them close together in rows onto a fabric base, creating a wonderful sea of ruffles. The different qualities, tones and textures of the ribbons I've chosen make this scarf even more exciting and glamorous.

You will need

Brown silk fabric – 90 x 12cm

Brown satin fabric – 90 x 12cm

Brown organza ribbon 80mm wide – 1.8m

Two lengths of brown satin ribbon 70mm wide – 1.8m

Brown wire-edged taffeta ribbon 70mm wide – 1.8m

Green/red shot wire-edged taffeta ribbon 70mm wide – 1.8m

Hook-and-eye fastening

1 Place the pieces of silk and satin fabrics with right sides together and pin. Machine-stitch a 1cm seam all the way around the edge, leaving an 8cm gap on one side. Clip the corners diagonally.

2 Turn the scarf right side out through the gap in the side seam. Turn in the seam allowance at the gap and press with a cool iron. Neatly hand-sew the gap together with slipstitch.

3 Take the five lengths of ribbon, turn both ends of each one over twice by 5mm and machine-stitch the hems down.

To stitch the gathering threads, loosen the tension on your sewing machine two notches and use the longest stitch. Sew a line down the centre of each ribbon, stopping at the halfway point and leaving a long thread. Then restart the line of stitching at this point and continue to the other end of the ribbon.

4 Fold the scarf in half to find the centre and mark this point with two pins. Starting with the organza ribbon as the middle ruffle, pin the centre of the ribbon, where the gathering threads meet, onto the centre point of the scarf.

Working on one half of the ribbon at a time, pull the bottom (bobbin) thread through to the top and use it to pull the gathers together gently until the ribbon is the same length as the scarf. Pin the ends of the ribbon to the scarf and secure the gathering threads by wrapping them around the pins in a figure-of-eight. Even out the gathers and pin the ribbon in place on the scarf every 3cm.

Using a small machine-stitch, sew over the gathering thread to attach the ribbon to the scarf. Backstitch the ends of the seam to secure them and trim away the excess threads at the figure-of-eight pins.

5 In the same way, gather and attach the two lengths of brown satin ribbon on either side of the organza ribbon, positioning them 2cm from the line of stitching down the centre of the organza ribbon.

6 Gather and sew on the two wire-edged taffeta ribbons, placing each one 1cm from the outer edge of the scarf. Lastly, sew a hook and eye to each end near the bottom edge of the scarf to fasten it.

Gold Evening Scarf

This idea of gathering up the ends of the scarf into a pouch shape was inspired by designs of the 1920s. The new silk extensions gather into a smaller bunch than the thicker fabric of the scarf would and give extra length, making the scarf more opulent. This is a good way to finish off the raw edges after cutting off an original tatty fringe.

You will need

Gold scarf – 40–45cm wide

Two pieces of gold silk – 20–30cm long and the width of the scarf plus 3cm for seams

Several gold and black embroidery beads – 2mm diameter

Four types of gold braids – lengths twice the width of the scarf plus 5cm for seams: I used gold braid with zigzag design 18mm wide, black and gold braid 43mm wide, gold satin braid 34mm wide and gold braid with knot design 18mm wide

Two gold tassels – 12cm long

1 If the scarf you are using has a fringe, cut it off. To make the silk extensions, first cut two pieces of silk between 20cm and 30cm long and the width of the scarf plus 3cm. Press the silk in half lengthways and then fold over and press a 1.5cm seam allowance at each end and a 1cm seam allowance along each long edge. With right sides together, pin one piece of silk to each raw end of the scarf and machine-stitch a 1cm seam to join them.

2 Press the seam towards the silk. Fold the silk so that the other pressed-under edge aligns with the seam you have just sewn. Pin in place. On the right side of the scarf, machine-stitch around the three edges of the silk extension.

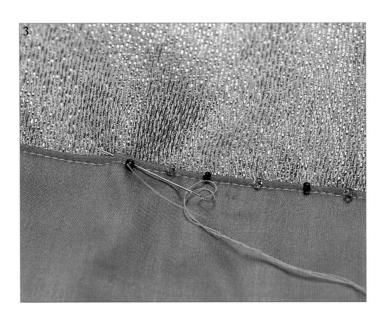

3 Sew a row of beads along the top edge of the silk, alternating gold beads with black beads and spacing them 1.5cm apart.

4 To attach the braids, leave a space of 10–12cm after the silk extension before pinning on the first braid, as otherwise it will be hidden in the gathers. Turn one end of the braid under by 2cm and pin it in position across the scarf, then cut the other end and turn it under as before. Measure the space from the scarf end to the braid carefully all the way along as you pin it in place to make sure the braid is completely straight. Machine-stitch along both edges of the braid to secure it.

Repeat to attach the other three braids, spacing them as you wish. I used the gold zigzag braid first, followed by the black and gold braid, the gold satin braid and finally the gold braid with the knot design.

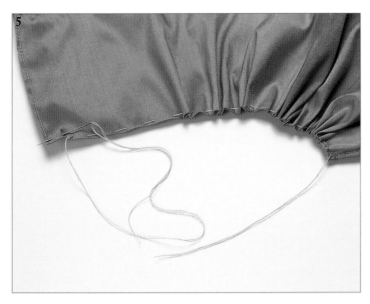

5 To gather the scarf ends, thread a needle with a double thread and knot the ends 10cm along. Work a backstitch, then continue to sew a line of running stitches 5mm in length along the bottom edge of the silk. Pull the stitches to gather up the bottom of the scarf. Knot the two thread ends together on the wrong side of the scarf to hold the gathers in place. Make a few stitches with the shorter thread end to secure it, then cut it, leaving the long thread in place.

6 A reasonably heavy beaded tassel works best for this scarf – the one I used was originally plain, but I stitched some beads onto it. Use the long thread still attached to the bottom of the scarf to sew the tassel securely in place. Thread the top of the tassel through the centre of the gathers and use at least four stitches on the wrong side of the scarf to hold it in place, then finish off the thread securely.

Repeat for the other end of the scarf.

Velvet Scarf with Organza Trim

As you gather this glistening gold and turquoise shot organza ribbon, the colours become more intense against the rich black velvet, as well as creating a sumptuous textured surface. You could use this wide scarf in the evenings to drape around your shoulders, or wear it during the day as a warm neck scarf.

You will need

Black crushed-velvet scarf – approximately 35cm wide

Gold/turquoise shot organza ribbon 105mm wide – a length four times the width of the scarf plus 16cm for hems and gathers

Turquoise silk – 10cm

Several matching embroidery beads – 2–3mm diameter

1 Turn the right-hand end of the organza ribbon under twice by 5mm and sew the hem in place with running stitch. Pull the stitches to gather up the end of the ribbon and secure it with some backstitches.

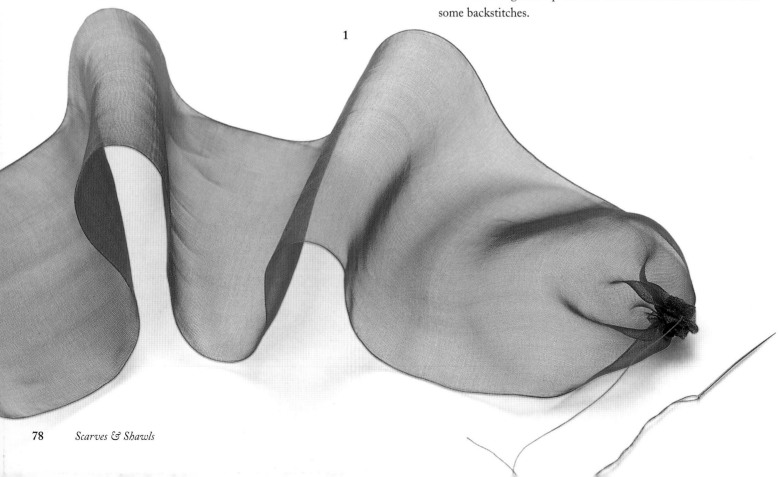

1

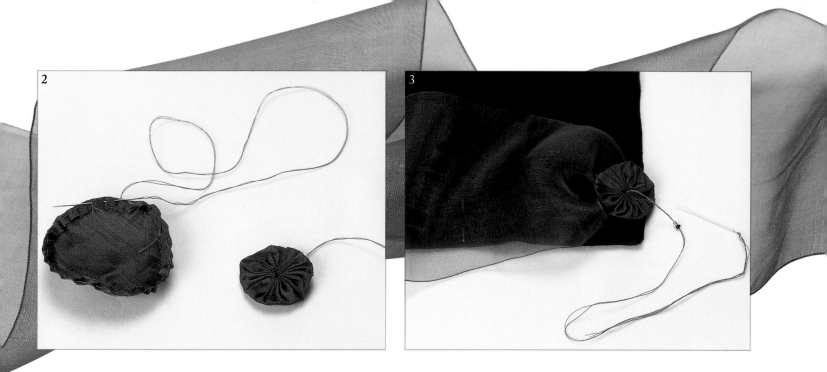

2 Cut out 14 circles from the turquoise silk, each with a diameter of 8cm. Referring to the instructions on page 19, make the Suffolk puffs out of the silk circles. Using a double thread knotted at the ends, fold the edge of the circle over by 5mm and secure the thread with a backstitch. Continue sewing running stitch around the circle, folding the edge over by 5mm as you sew. Pull the thread to gather up the stitches into a tight circle and form the puff, then secure the gathers with a backstitch. Don't cut the thread.

3 Sew the organza ribbon and Suffolk puffs across the end of the scarf. To do this, pin the gathered end of the organza ribbon in place on the right-hand end of the velvet scarf, 5cm up from the bottom edge. Using the thread attached to the Suffolk puff, sew it down over the gathered organza in several places. Try not to sew through the lining of the scarf so that the stitches remain invisible. Sew some beads into the centre of the Suffolk puff, then finish off the thread with some backstitches on the underside to secure it.

4 Repeat this process to attach the rest of the organza ribbon and the other Suffolk puffs across the end of the scarf. Work out how many puffs you will need and how far apart you want to space them, then mark these points on the velvet with a pin – this will depend on the width of your scarf. I used four spaced about 10cm apart. At each marker pin gather the organza ribbon using the thread attached to each Suffolk puff before you sew the puff in place. When you reach the left-hand end of the scarf, hem the end of the organza ribbon in the same way as you did at the start, before sewing the last Suffolk puff in place.

Create a second row of organza ribbon and Suffolk puffs 10cm above the first, starting and finishing the row 10cm in from the ends. Use three puffs and place them in alternate spaces to those in the row below. Sew some beads at both ends of this shorter row.

Repeat on the other end of the scarf.

White Mohair Scarf

This glamorous mohair scarf can be worn as a wrap in the evening or as a cosy neck warmer on crisp days, teamed with the matching gloves on page 40. It's a luxurious and romantic look that conjures up images of falling snowflakes and walks through frosty parks. The gathered-ribbon technique is so simple to do but looks really special.

You will need

White mohair scarf – approximately 50cm wide

White braid 15mm wide – a length twice the width of the scarf plus 6cm for hems

White fur trim 75mm wide – a length twice the width of the scarf

Ivory satin ribbon 25mm wide – a length six times the width of the scarf

14 crystal beads – 4mm diameter

1 To attach the first row of 15mm-wide white braid to the scarf, thread a needle with double thread and knot the ends. Fold one end of the braid under by 1.5cm and stitch it down at one edge of the scarf, 1cm in from the end. Pin the remaining length of braid across the scarf, making sure it is positioned exactly 1cm in from the end of the scarf all the way along. Hand-sew it in place with running stitch through the centre of the braid.

2 Cut a length of fur trim to the width of your scarf and pin into place just above the first row of braid. Holding the fur fibres out of the way, sew the trim to the scarf along the top and bottom edges. Oversew the ends of the trim and the scarf together.

3 Cut a length of ivory ribbon three times the width of your scarf and fold one end under by 5mm. Thread a needle with double thread and knot the ends. Sew this hem down with a line of running stitches. Work a backstitch, then sew a line of running stitches in a zigzag pattern along the length of the ribbon.

4 Gather the ribbon up as you go. When you reach the end, turn under 5mm and, making sure the ruched ribbon is the right length to fit the width of the scarf exactly, finish off with a backstitch to secure the gathers and sew down the hem.

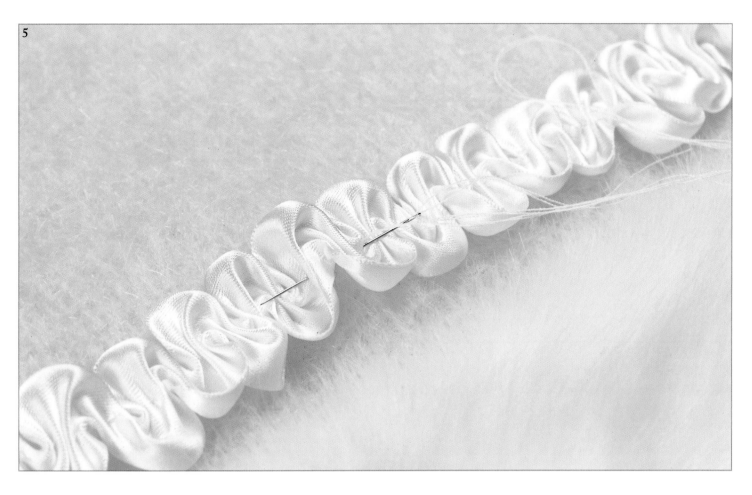

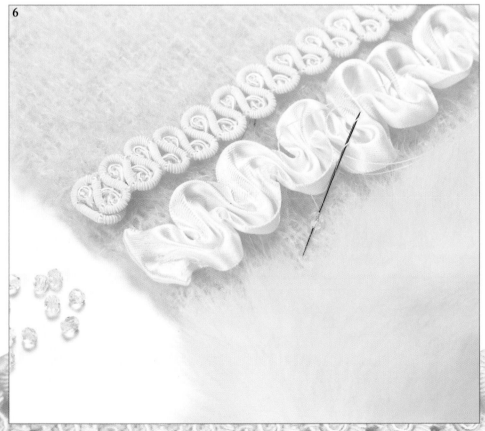

5 Pin the ruched ribbon to the scarf just above the top of the fur trim and sew it in place with running stitch.

6 Sew a second row of braid to the scarf above the ruched ribbon in the same way as the first.

Sew seven beads on between the ribbon and the fur. To do this, secure a double thread on the wrong side of the scarf with a backstitch, leaving a long end. Take the needle through to the front and thread a bead on. Stitch through to the wrong side of the scarf and knot the ends of the threads together to secure them.

Trim the other end of the scarf in the same way as the first.

Bags & Baskets

Little Summer Basket

There are many exciting raffia braids available, but I chose this lovely woven yellow, as it matched the taffeta ribbon that reminds me of sherbet lemons, and a toning narrow raffia fringe. The summery colours make this the perfect basket for a promenade along the seafront or a summer lunch al fresco. Complete the look with the matching haircomb on page 34.

You will need

Small basket – approximately 65cm circumference

Yellow woven raffia 35mm wide – 70cm

Raffia fringe 25mm wide – 70cm

Orange gingham ribbon 5mm wide – 70cm

Yellow striped ribbon 25mm wide – 2.5m

Orange and yellow embroidery beads – 2mm diameter

Two orange beads – 5mm diameter

1 Start with the length of yellow woven raffia. Thread the needle with matching thread, doubling it over and knotting the ends. Secure the thread with several stitches at one end of the raffia, then turn under 2.5cm and sew this end down, taking care not to let the stitches show on the right side.

Starting at one side of the basket, use running stitch to sew the raffia around the basket, positioning it so it just overlaps the rim and keeping your line of stitches in the centre of the raffia. Use a thimble to help you push the needle through. You may need to lift the raffia to see where to place your stitch in the basket – just make sure you pull the stitches quite tightly once the raffia is laid down. Stitches should be about 2.5cm apart – use the pattern on the raffia as a guide. Thread a small orange bead onto the front of each stitch – this is a good way to hide the stitches on the outside of the basket. When you reach the point where you started, turn under 2.5cm and sew the hem in place. Then sew the two ends of the raffia together.

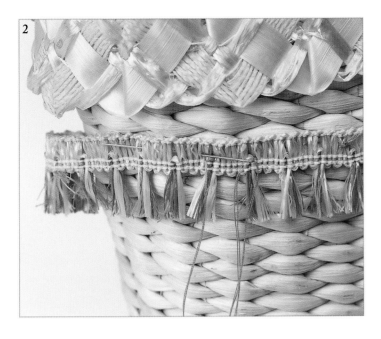

2 Next take the raffia fringe and hem the end. Sew the fringe around the bag under the woven raffia in the same way. It doesn't matter if the stitches show, as they will be covered by the gingham ribbon in the next step.

3 Take a length of orange gingham ribbon and sew it on top of the raffia fringe, using a matching single thread and small running stitches. Thread a yellow bead onto the front of each small stitch – there is no need to sew right through to the basket.

4 Follow the instructions on page 18 to make two ribbon rosettes, using 50cm-lengths of yellow striped ribbon for each one. Sew on one rosette at each end of your basket with a large orange bead in the centre.

Emerald Beaded Bag

This bag is a simple shape to make and is lined the way I line all my bags, resulting in a perfect finish around the top edge. The emerald-green beaded fringe is the star ingredient and I kept everything else green to give it unity, while enjoying the contrast of different ribbons. This bag should be heavily beaded, so sew on as many beads as you like.

You will need

Green satin fabric – 20cm

Ultra-soft iron-on backing – 20cm

Green beaded fringe with 7.5cm drop – 36cm

Green silk ribbon 15mm wide – 36cm

Gold-edged green organza 35mm wide – 36cm

Green velvet ribbon 35mm – 36cm

Green velvet ribbon 5mm wide – 36cm

Three velvet ribbons in different shades of green 5mm wide – 1m of each

Button or bead – 1–1.5cm diameter

Button elastic

1 Make a paper pattern, 18 x 39cm, using the template on page 153. Mark the centre fold line (this will be the bottom of the bag). Using the pattern, cut out two pieces of green satin and one of iron-on backing.

Following the manufacturer's instructions, iron the backing onto the wrong side of one piece of satin. This is your outer bag fabric; the other piece of satin, without the backing, is the lining fabric.

2 To attach the beaded fringe, start at one edge of the outer bag fabric and place a row of beaded fringe 2cm from the top. Ensure that the tape reaches each side edge, but carefully remove the end strings of beads and put them to one side. Pin the fringe in place and machine-stitch along the top edge of the tape.

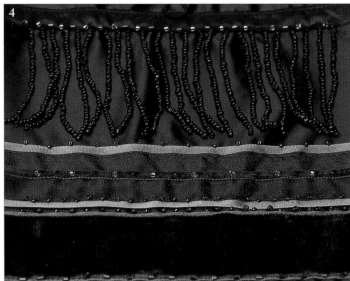

3 Machine-stitch the length of silk ribbon over the tape to cover it. Next, pin in place and machine-stitch the gold-edged organza 11cm down from the top edge. Sew over the green part of the ribbon, not the gold. Then sew the wide velvet ribbon on below the organza. Sew the narrow velvet ribbon through the centre of the organza.

Repeat the pattern at the other end of the fabric, starting with the beaded fringe. There should be a gap of about 1.5cm between the two wide velvet ribbons in the centre of the fabric.

4 Using a double thread knotted at the ends, work several backstitches on the wrong side and then sew rows of beads along the edges of the ribbons. Don't sew any beads closer than 1cm to the edges of the fabric, as they will get caught in the side seams.

Sew a loop of elastic for the button in the centre of one top edge.

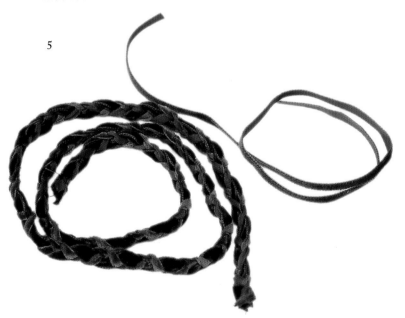

5 The bag handle is made by plaiting three strips of 5mm-wide velvet ribbon, each 1m long. Secure the three ribbons one on top of the other at one end with a safety pin and hold this in place under the sewing-machine foot. To make the plait, take each ribbon in turn into the centre, making sure you keep the right side of the velvet to the top of the plait.

6 To make up the bag, fold the outer bag fabric in half with right sides together, keeping the beaded fringe out of the way. Pin and machine-stitch a 1cm seam along both sides.

Do the same with the lining, leaving a gap of 10cm in the stitching on the right-hand side seam.

Clip the corners diagonally and turn the bag right side out.

7 Pin the ends of the plaited handle to the outer bag at the side seams, lining up the ends of the handle with the top edge of the bag, then machine-stitch in place to attach the handle securely.

8 Insert the outer bag into the lining so the right sides are together and then pin and machine-stitch around the top edge. Turn the bag right side out through the gap in the side seam of the lining, turning the lining right side out at the same time. Turn in the 1cm hem allowance and then pin and machine-stitch the gap in the lining, finishing off the threads securely.

9 Push the lining into the bag and finish by machine-stitching a line of topstitch around the opening of the bag to create a neat edge.

Sew the button onto the centre of the top edge opposite the elastic loop. Then sew beads around all the edges of the bag.

Clutch Bag

The design of this bag is based on one I inherited from my great-grandmother, which is blue velvet with several rows of diamanté across the front flap. You can decorate the flap with anything you like – more beads, ruched ribbon or fabric, or some vintage lace or braid – you only need a little piece, so use something extra-special.

You will need

Navy blue velvet – 40cm

Navy blue taffeta lining fabric – 30cm

Iron-on interfacing – 30cm

Blue/green tartan ribbon 25mm wide – 22cm

Gold-edged navy blue organza ribbon 25mm wide – 22cm

Green silk ribbon 15mm wide – 22cm

Selection of blue and green beads – 2mm diameter

Press-stud fastening

1 Use the template on page 154 to make a pattern and cut out one piece each of velvet, taffeta and interfacing. It is very important that when you cut out the velvet you place the shot side of the pattern parallel to the selvedge, as otherwise the pile of the velvet will be going in opposite directions on the front and the flap of the bag.

Following the manufacturer's instructions, iron the interfacing onto the wrong side of the piece of navy blue velvet.

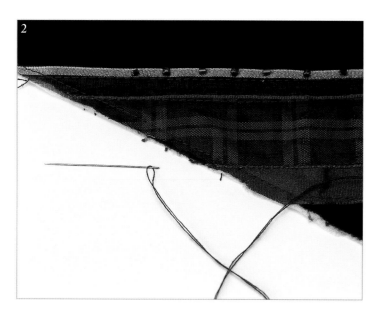

2 Pin the strips of ribbon across the narrow section of the velvet, starting 3cm up with the green silk and finishing 1cm below the end of the diagonal with the gold-edged organza. Overlap each ribbon and leave the ends overhanging at the diagonal edge. Machine-stitch in place. Cut the ribbons along the diagonal edge and sew along this edge to hold the ends in place.

Sew on two rows of beads, one along the gold-edged organza and one along the green silk ribbon, alternating blue and green beads and leaving a space of 1.5cm at the ends for the seams.

3 Place the taffeta lining fabric on the velvet with right sides together and pin it in place. Machine-stitch around the edge, but leave a gap of 12cm in the stitching on the long side.

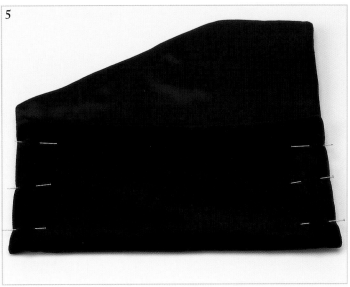

4 Clip the corners diagonally, being careful not to cut the stitching, then turn the bag right side out. Press the seam allowances in at the gap and press all the edges flat, ironing the lining not the velvet.

5 Fold the bottom edge of the bag up by 11.5cm and pin it along the sides. Take care to keep all the layers of fabric pinned in place at the gap. Begin to machine-stitch 1cm up from the folded edge and sew down towards it. Pivot at the folded edge and stitch back up to the opening. Finish the machine threads at the folded edge by hand-sewing them in place.

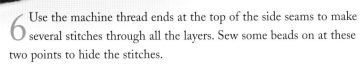

6 Use the machine thread ends at the top of the side seams to make several stitches through all the layers. Sew some beads on at these two points to hide the stitches.

7 Sew a press-stud fastening to the lining at the base of the flap, making sure you don't sew through the velvet, and in the corresponding place on the front of the bag.

Shopping Basket

I decorated this wicker shopping basket with six large Suffolk puffs, with a beaded ribbon rosette in the centre of each. I also trimmed the top edge with some lovely striped grosgrain and a narrow ribbon in toning colours. There are lots of plain baskets around that offer scope for decoration to make them look very special.

You will need

Large wicker shopping basket

Cream ribbon with red edging 5mm wide – a length measuring the circumference of the top of the basket plus 1.5cm

Red and white striped grosgrain ribbon 20mm wide – length as above

Calico fabric – 30cm

Brown, cream and red checked wire-edged taffeta ribbon 38mm wide – 4m

Eight wooden beads or buttons – 5mm diameter

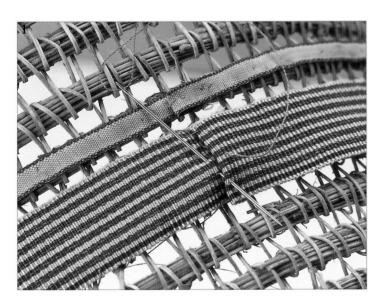

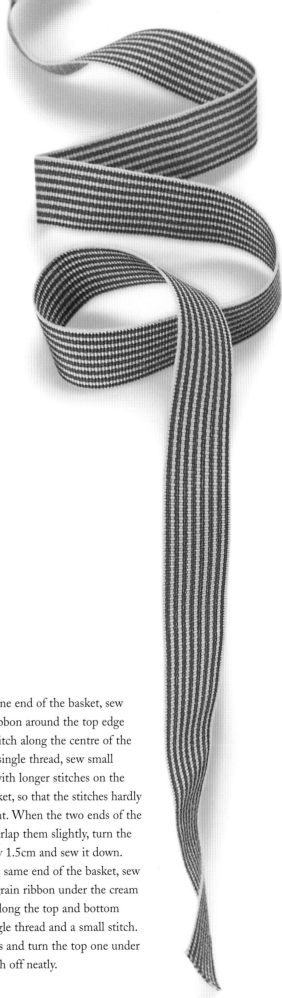

1 Starting at one end of the basket, sew the cream ribbon around the top edge using running stitch along the centre of the ribbon. Using a single thread, sew small stitches on top with longer stitches on the inside of the basket, so that the stitches hardly show on the front. When the two ends of the ribbon meet, overlap them slightly, turn the top end under by 1.5cm and sew it down.

Starting at the same end of the basket, sew the striped grosgrain ribbon under the cream ribbon, sewing along the top and bottom edges with a single thread and a small stitch. Overlap the ends and turn the top one under as before to finish off neatly.

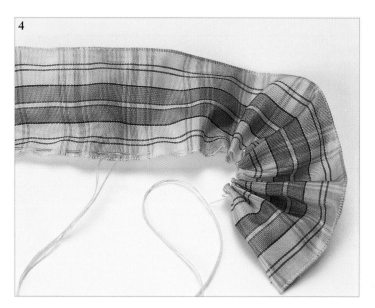

2 Make six Suffolk puffs (see also instructions on page 19). To do this, first cut six circles of calico, 22cm in diameter – a small plate makes a good template to draw around. Using a double thread knotted at the ends, fold over the edge of the circle by 5mm and secure with a backstitch. Sew running stitch around the edge of the circle, folding the edge of the fabric over by 5mm as you sew.

3 Pull the thread firmly to gather up the stitches into a tight circle and form the calico puff. Secure the thread with a backstitch to hold the gathers in place.

4 For the ribbon rosettes (see also page 18), first remove the wire from the bottom edge of the checked taffeta ribbon. Turn one end of the ribbon under by 5mm and, starting with a backstitch, sew the hem in place. Then sew a line of running stitches along the bottom edge of the ribbon, starting to gather it up gently as you go.

5 Once you reach the other end of the ribbon, pull the gathering thread firmly but gently to form a circle. Turn under a 5mm hem at the other end of the ribbon and sew it down. Then sew the two ends of the ribbon together. Don't cut the thread.

6 Use the same thread to sew the rosette into the centre of the Suffolk puff, threading a bead on at the same time. Use at least four stitches and go right through to the basket to secure it.

Make five more Suffolk puffs and beaded ribbon rosettes in the same way, and then attach three to the front and three to the back of the basket beneath the grosgrain ribbon.

7 Make two more ribbon rosettes in the same way as before and sew them, with a bead in the centre of each, onto the middle of the grosgrain ribbon at both sides of the basket, covering the join in the ribbons at one side.

Tasselled Bag

Drawstring bags have been around for ever, as this is the simplest way of making a bag that closes securely. There are two separate lengths of ribbon, one for each handle. I love the contrast of the black velvet and the rich turquoise lining as you open the bag.

You will need

Black velvet – 30cm

Turquoise silk – 30cm

Turquoise satin ribbon 25mm wide – 1.2m

Black sparkly tassel – approximately 12cm long

Selection of matching beads – 2–3mm diameter

1 Using the template on page 155, make a U-shaped paper pattern measuring 30cm across the top and 26cm deep. Pin the pattern to the fabric and cut out two pieces in black velvet and two in silk. Make sure the pile on the velvet runs in the same direction on both pieces.

Working 10cm down from the top edge, sew groups of three beads onto both pieces of velvet.

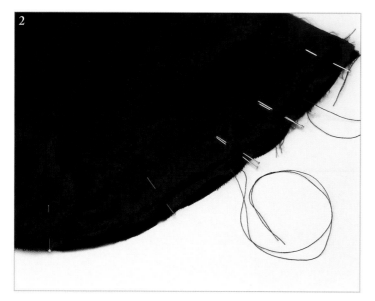

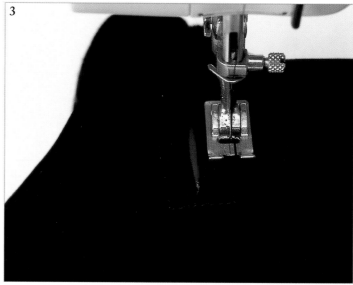

2 Place the two pieces of black velvet with right sides together. Sandwich the tassel between the two halves, positioning the top of the tassel centrally on the bottom edge of the bag with the tail of the tassel pointing up inside the bag. Pin in place.

Use two pins to mark the gaps in the side seams that will form the casing for the drawstring ribbon. To do this, measure 7cm down from the top edge and pin, then measure a further 3.5cm down and pin. You will not sew between these two points.

3 Machine-stitch a 1.5cm seam around the sides and bottom of the bag. Reverse-stitch when you stop and start on each side of the pins marking the opening for the drawstring casing.

Open out the seam allowance at the gap in the seam and sew zigzag stitch on the machine along the raw edges to 1cm above and below the openings. Using a straight machine-stitch, sew the seam allowance down flat along the sides of the opening and then sew across the top and bottom of the gap to form a rectangle.

4 To make up the lining, pin the two pieces of turquoise silk with right sides together. Machine-stitch a 1cm seam around the edge, leaving a central gap of 12cm at the bottom.

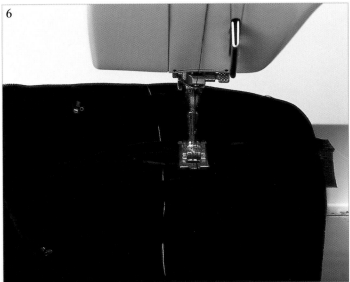

5 Turn the velvet outer bag right side out and place it inside the lining, with right sides together. Pin and machine-stitch a 1.5cm seam around the top edge.

Pull the outer bag through the gap in the bottom of the lining and then sew up the gap, turning the seam allowance under and machine-stitching on the right side of the lining. Push the lining inside the bag and topstitch around the top edge of the bag.

6 To make the casing for the drawstring ribbons, first pin the lining to the bag at the side seams level with the two openings. Pin and then tack the lining to the bag at this point all the way around.

Measure the distance from the top of the bag to the top of the side opening to work out your seam width and mark this on your machine with sticky tape. Measure the distance from the bottom of the opening to the top of the bag and mark it on your machine in the same way. Machine-stitch both these seams in place. Then remove the tacking stitches.

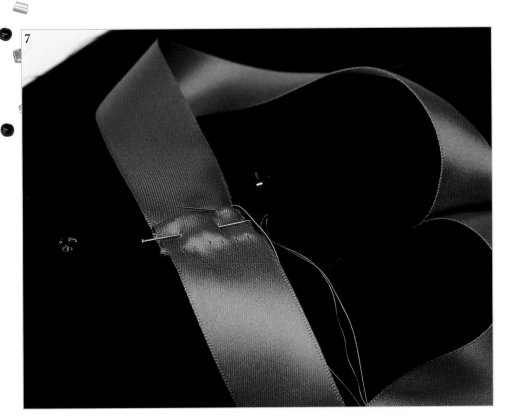

7 For the ribbon handles, cut the length of turquoise ribbon in two. Secure a safety pin at one end of the ribbon and use this to feed one length of ribbon into one slit. Work it all the way through the casing and bring it out again through the same slit. Feed the other length of ribbon into the other slit and work it all the way through the casing as before.

Overlap the ends of the ribbons, turning the raw ends under, and hand-sew them together. Pull both of the ribbons through the casing a little way so that the seams are hidden inside.

Finish by sewing a row of beads around the top edge of the bag.

Clothes & Cover-ups

Summer Dress with Tiered Skirt

I knew I would find a use for this pretty pink and yellow ribbon the moment I saw it. When I came across the dress, I decided that loops of ribbon would work well on the full skirt and really show off the ribbon. The different sections of the dress provide lots of opportunity for decoration, so I went to town with toning pinks and yellows. The matching pumps and stole on pages 52 and 66 complete the outfit.

You will need

Tiered white cotton dress

Yellow organza ribbon 40mm wide – sufficient to go around the hem of the dress (I used 4.4m), plus 1m for the bows on the shoulder straps

Pink silk/satin ribbon 15mm wide – sufficient to go around the hem of the dress

Yellow organza ribbon 21mm wide – sufficient to sew around the V-shaped neckline and the hips

Pink silk/satin ribbon 9mm wide – length as above

Yellow embroidery beads – 2mm diameter

Pink satin ribbon 40mm wide – three times the circumference of the dress at the point where the rosebud trim will be sewn on)

Pearl beads – 3mm diameter

Pink/yellow taffeta ribbon 24mm wide – 5.5m

Yellow organza ribbon 36mm wide – 7m

Clear nail varnish

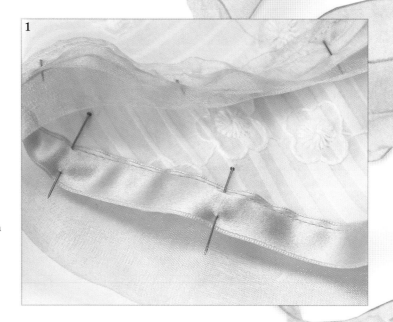

1 Sew the 40mm-wide yellow organza ribbon around the hem of the dress so that it overlaps the bottom edge by 5mm. Start at one of the side seams and pin then machine-stitch the ribbon to the wrong side of the dress. Fold the ends under and hand-sew them in place.

Sew the 15mm-wide pink silk/satin ribbon onto the right side of the dress at the hem. It should cover the dress fabric and overlap onto the organza by 3mm. Machine-stitch along both edges of the ribbon.

2 Pin and then machine-stitch the 21mm-wide yellow organza ribbon to the wrong side of the dress at the neckline, overhanging the edge by 16mm. Tuck the ends of the ribbon under the shoulder straps, turn the ends under and hand-sew them in place.

Sew some 9mm-wide pink silk/satin ribbon to the outside of the dress at the neckline. Turn the ends under and hand-sew them in place.

3 Make a folded ribbon bow to decorate the V of the neckline. To do this, cut a piece of 9mm-wide pink silk/satin ribbon 9cm long and fold it so that the two ends meet and overlap in the centre. Pin then hand-stitch in place.

4 Pull the stitches up to gather the bow in the centre. Then use the same thread to sew the bow onto the dress, threading three small yellow beads onto the centre of the bow.

5 Use the 40mm-wide pink satin ribbon to make the rosebud trim. Lay the ribbon horizontally on your work surface. Measuring from left to right, put a pin in the ribbon 5cm from the end. Put another pin in the ribbon 7cm along from the first pin. Measure 4cm along and put in a third pin. Repeat another four times until you have five 7cm sections.

6

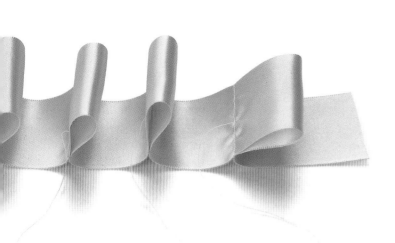

6 Bring the pins together at each end of the 7cm sections and pin horizontally. Starting in the centre of the ribbon width, machine-stitch in reverse up to the top edge. Then sew down to the bottom edge of the ribbon and reverse back up to the centre.

7

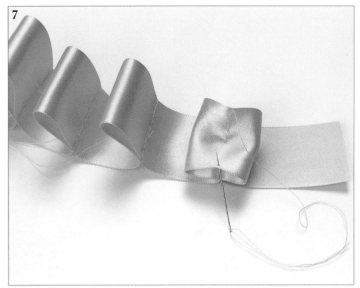

7 Cut off three of the four thread ends. Thread the remaining strand into a needle and pull it up through the centre of the fold onto the right side of the ribbon. Sew two or three stitches from the centre up to the top edge of the ribbon. Now stitch into the bottom edge of the ribbon and sew two or three stitches back to the centre.

8

8 Push the needle out at the back of the ribbon and pull the stitches up to gather into a rosebud. Work a few stitches to hold the gathers in place and then sew a small pearl bead onto the front of the rosebud. Finish the thread off securely at the back.

Continue along the ribbon until you have enough rosebuds to go around the dress. Alternate yellow and pearl beads.

9

9 Pin the rosebud ribbon trim around the dress, just above the hips about 6cm below the waist, and hand-sew it on along both the top and bottom edges. Turn the raw end under by 1cm and hand-sew it in place.

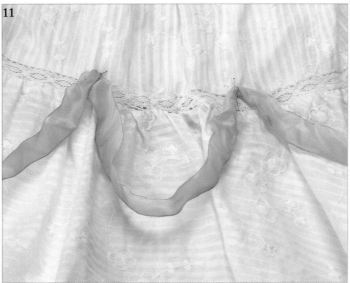

10 Sew a row of 21mm-wide yellow organza ribbon and 9mm-wide pink satin ribbon above the rosebud trim. Place the pink satin ribbon on top of the yellow organza and pin them in place around the dress, 2mm above the rosebud trim. Machine-stitch them to the dress along the top and bottom edges of the pink satin ribbon. Turn the ends under by 1cm and hand-sew in place.

11 For the ribbon swags, use pins to mark ten points equal distances apart, just above the first tier of the dress. Start at one of the side seams and pin one end of the pink/yellow taffeta ribbon in place, turning it under first by 1cm. Measure 30cm along the ribbon and pin in place at the next marker pin. Continue until you have uniform loops pinned in place all around the skirt.

12 Following the instructions on pages 14–15, make ten bows using 70cm lengths of 36mm-wide yellow organza ribbon. Cut the ends of the ribbons diagonally and paint them with clear nail varnish to prevent them from fraying. Using a double thread knotted at the ends, stitch into the taffeta ribbon where it is pinned to the dress at the top of each swag and sew several stitches to secure it. Remove the pin and sew the organza bow on top, making sure you stitch through all the layers of the knot. Thread a pearl bead onto the last stitch to hide it. Finish the thread off on the inside of the dress.

13 For the bows on the shoulder straps, cut two 50cm lengths of both the 24mm-wide pink/yellow taffeta and the 40mm-wide yellow organza. Place the taffeta on top of the organza and tie two bows as before (see pages 14–15). Sew the bows to the front base of the shoulder straps in the same way as you attached the organza bows, adding a single pearl bead to the last stitch and securing the thread on the inside of the strap.

Shocking-pink Dancing Dress

*I love the colour and 1950s style of this dress, and adding the black
ribbon frill to the lining creates the effect of the era's stiff petticoats.
The matching black sash, with ruched ribbon detail at the ends, makes
a striking contrast to the pink. The addition of the black organza and
satin at the neckline ties the whole dress together.*

You will need

Full-skirted pink dress with a full lining

For the frill:

Black organza ribbon 100mm wide – twice
the circumference of the lining hem
(a good length would be about 6m)

Black satin ribbon 50mm wide – length
as above

For the sash:

Black satin ribbon 65mm wide – 4m

Black satin ribbon 35mm wide – 1m

Bright pink silk – 10 x 20cm

Two crystal beads – 5mm diameter

Clear nail varnish

For the neckline:

Black organza ribbon 100mm wide – 18cm

Black satin ribbon 35mm wide – 18cm

For the shoes:

Bright pink silk – 10 x 20cm

Two crystal beads – 5mm diameter

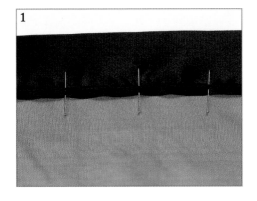

1 To make the frill, place the organza
ribbon on top of the 50mm-wide satin
ribbon, overlapping the edges by 6mm. Pin
and machine-stitch them together.

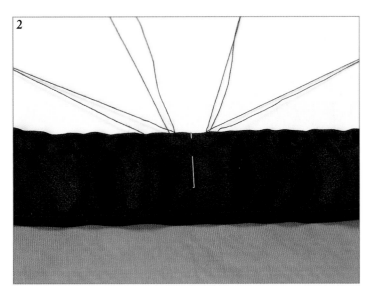

2 Don't cut the ribbons but divide this long length into four equal lengths and mark each
section with a pin. Do the same with the hem of the dress lining. Each quarter section
of the ribbon will be gathered onto a quarter section of the lining. Next, sew a double line of
gathering threads along the top of the satin ribbon. To do this, set the machine to a long stitch
length and loosen the tension. Leaving long threads at the beginning and end, stitch two lines
of gathers 1cm apart along each quarter section, leaving a 2cm space at both ends of the ribbon.

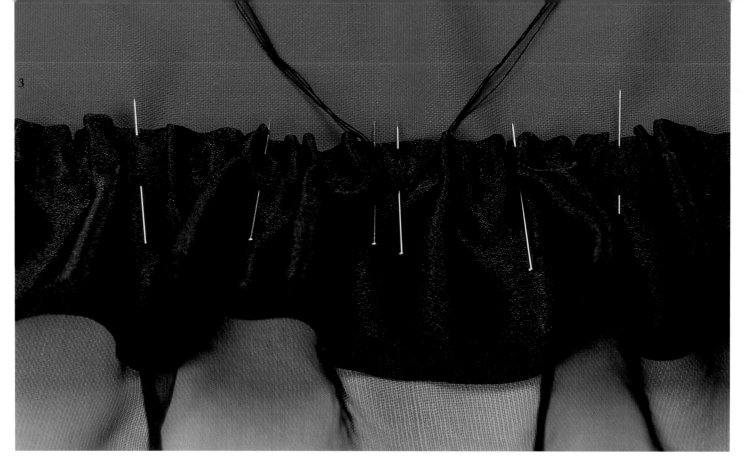

3 Starting at the centre back, pin one end of the frill right side up to the hem of the lining (so the right side of the frill will face outwards on the finished dress). Pin in the same way at the next quarter mark. Pull the bobbin (underneath) threads through to the right side and gently gather the ribbon frill, working from both ends of the section. When the gathered frill looks roughly the same length as the lining, wind the threads (top and bottom) at one end of the section in a figure-of-eight around the pin. Spread the gathers evenly and, once you are satisfied that the frill is the same length as the lining, secure the threads at the other end of the section in

a figure-of-eight around the pin there. Pin the gathered section of the frill in place about 1.5cm above the hem of the lining. Use your fingers to feel if it is in place, then turn it over and check. Repeat this on each of the other three sections. When you reach the end of the frill, turn the raw ends under by 1.5cm and overlap them.

Using a small machine-stitch, sew the frill to the lining, stitching between the two lines of gathering threads.

Remove the pins and cut off all the long threads from the gathering stitches. Use a single thread to hand-sew the two ends of the frill together and oversew the raw edges.

4 To make the sash, cut the length of 65mm-wide satin ribbon in half and stitch the two strips together along their length, placing one on top of the other with an overlap of 6mm. You may wish to pin it in place, but don't machine-stitch over a pin as it will mark the satin. Cut both ends of the joined ribbons diagonally and paint them with clear nail varnish to prevent them from fraying.

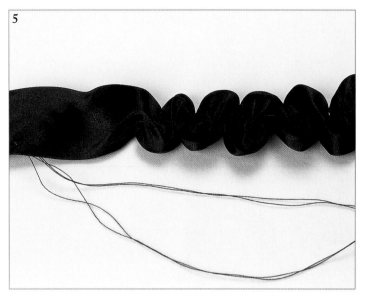

5 To decorate the ends of the sash, cut a 50cm length of 35mm-wide satin ribbon and ruche it (see also page 15). Thread a needle with a double thread and knot the ends. Turn one end of the ribbon under by 5mm and sew it in place. Make a backstitch and sew a line of running stitches along the ribbon in a zigzag pattern as shown. As you go, gently pull the stitches to gather up the ribbon. Continue to the end of the ribbon, leaving 5mm to turn under. Gather the ribbon to fit the width of the end of the sash, then sew a backstitch to secure the gathers.

6 Sew the hem of the ribbon under, then use the same thread to stitch the ruched ribbon band onto the end of the sash. Make sure it covers the bottom edge, but don't worry if the corner shows as there will be a Suffolk puff to cover it. Repeat the above for the other end of the sash.

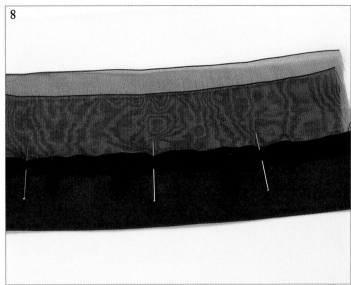

7 Cut two 8cm-diameter circles out of the bright pink silk and make two Suffolk puffs to sew onto each end of the sash (see page 19). To sew them on, take the thread through to the back of the puff and then sew them onto the end of the sash. Thread a crystal bead onto the thread and stitch through to the back of the sash. Bring the thread through the sash and finish off with a backstitch under the puff, so the stitches don't show on the underside of the sash.

8 To tie in the neckline with the hemline of the dress, sew a piece of organza and satin into the V-neck. To do this, take an 18cm length of 100mm-wide organza ribbon and fold it horizontally, so that there is 1cm at the top between the edges, and pin it in place. Then, with the organza on top, machine-stitch the folded edge to an 18cm length of 35mm-wide satin ribbon.

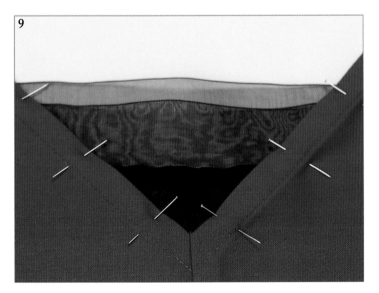

9 Place this piece in the V-neck of the dress, with the right side of the ribbon to the wrong side of the dress. It is best to do this while wearing the dress to ensure that you achieve the right tension across the top of the organza. Pin it in place on the right side of the dress, making sure there is plenty of overlap on the inside. Take off the dress and machine-stitch the trim in place, sewing on the outside of the dress using matching pink thread. Trim away the excess ribbons on the inside of the neckline and hem the edges by hand.

10 Cut two more 8cm-diameter circles out of the bright pink silk and make two more Suffolk puffs. Sew them onto the front of your shoes to match them to your dress, finishing off with a crystal bead in the centre of the puff as before.

Pencil Skirt with Braided Hem

As an alternative to trimming clothes by sewing on straight rows of ribbons or braids, you can create all sorts of geometrical patterns by stitching and folding them onto fabric. This zigzag design around the hem of a pencil skirt is simple to do, but very striking. Make a matching belt using wide embroidered linen tape (see page 36).

You will need

Knee-length beige pencil skirt

Cream braid with turquoise stitching 5mm
wide – a length twice the circumference
of the skirt hem plus 6cm for hems

Turquoise braid 15mm wide – a length twice
the circumference of the skirt hem plus
20cm for hems and folds

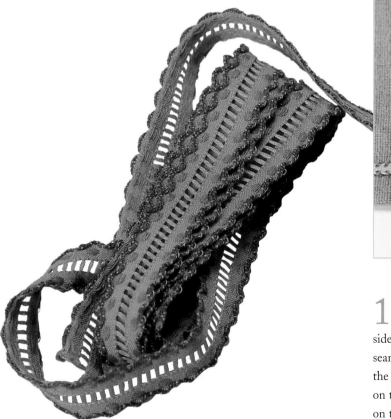

1 First sew the narrow cream braid onto the skirt. If the skirt has a lining, fold it up out of the way. If there is a slit at the back or side, start the braid on the inside of this; if there is no slit, start at a seam. Fold the raw end under and sew the braid along the bottom of the skirt 1cm from the edge, using running stitch with a small stitch on top and a longer one underneath so that the stitches hardly show on the right side of the skirt.

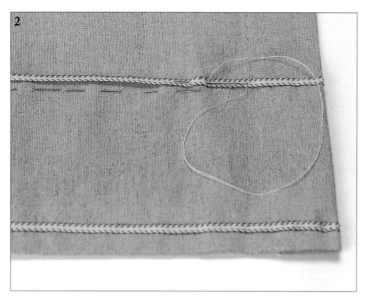

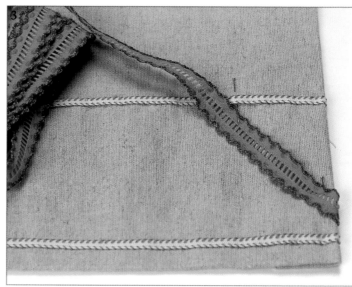

2 Use pins to mark a line 8cm above the first row of braid. Attach another row of the same braid just above this line of pins, sewing it on with running stitch in the same way as before.

3 Use the turquoise braid to create the zigzag design. Starting at the slit or seam of your skirt and working from right to left, tuck the raw end of the braid under and pin it in place. Measure 4.5cm along the top row of cream braid from the slit or seam and mark this point with a pin. Bring the turquoise braid up diagonally to the meet the cream braid at this point.

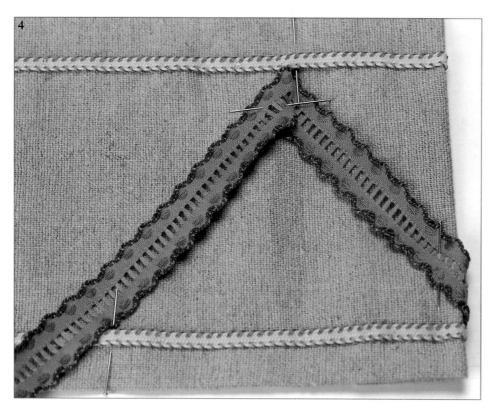

4 Hold the turquoise braid at the marked point and fold the left-hand side so that when the fold lies flat it is vertical and the design on the braid meets up. You will have created a double folded triangle underneath. Now bring the turquoise braid down diagonally to the bottom row of cream braid, leaving a 9cm space at the base of the triangle between the two turquoise strips. Pin the top fold in place, positioning the pins horizontally so they won't get caught in the sewing machine later.

5 Repeat the fold in the turquoise braid at the bottom row of cream braid, bringing it up to the top row again to make another V-shape. Continue this process until you have pinned the turquoise braid all the way around the skirt between the two rows of cream braid. You may need to adjust the width of your zigzags slightly as you reach the end, so that you can join the pattern at the slit or seam.

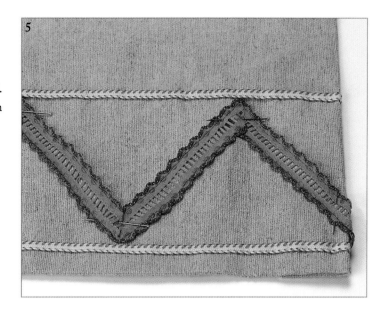

6 Machine-stitch along both edges of the turquoise braid to hold it in place, lifting the presser foot with the needle still in the fabric and pivoting the fabric to sew around each V-point.

Turn the end of the braid under and use the long threads at the seam ends to stitch it down on the inside of the slit if there is one.

Lightly press the skirt on the wrong side.

Circular Wrapover Skirt

I made my first circular skirt at the age of 14 out of a beautiful white cotton sheet that had belonged to my grandmother. I trimmed the hem with a vintage duck-egg blue braid and wore it with red tie-up espadrilles. I've made lots of circular skirts since, and this one is decorated with brightly coloured couched-on cords, which look stunning against black cotton.

You will need

Black cotton fabric – 4 x 1.9m

Iron-on interfacing – 94 x 8cm

Two hook-and-eye fastenings

Red, blue and green ribbons 7mm wide –
    8m of each

Coloured cord in seven colours – 3m of each

Seven circles of fabric to match the cords –
    8cm diameter

Three beads to match each circle – 2–3mm

1 To cut out the skirt, follow the diagram and instructions on page 152. Join the two semicircles of the skirt by sewing the two selvedges together. Open out the seam and press. Sew a line of machine-stitching around the curve of the waistline, 1cm down from the cut edge, to prevent it from stretching.

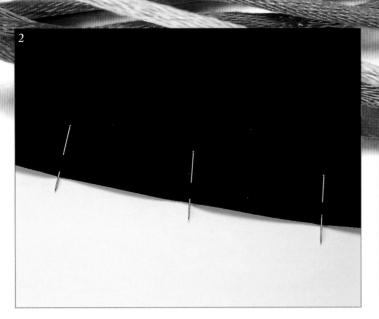

2 Turn under and press first 1cm then another 1cm hem around the bottom of the skirt. Machine-stitch the hem down. Fold under and press the two selvedges and machine them in place.

3 Iron the interfacing onto the wrong side of the waistband, lining it up with the cut edge.

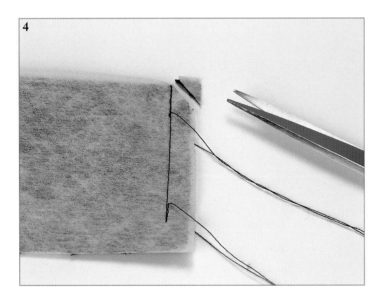

4 Fold the waistband in half with right sides together and press. Machine-stitch the ends, starting and stopping 1.5cm in from the edges. Clip the corners diagonally.

5 Turn the waistband right side out and press. Place the fabric side of the interfaced part of the waistband next to the right side of the skirt at the waistline and pin. Machine-stitch in place.

Turn right side out and press with the seam towards the waistband.

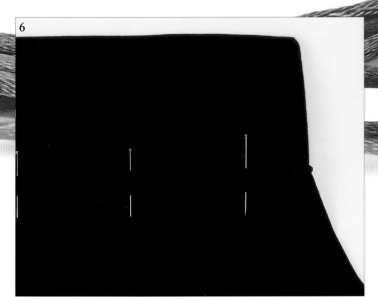

6 On the inside of the skirt, pin the selvedge of the waistband over the seamline. From the right side, machine-stitch it in place along the edge of the waistband.

The right side of the skirt overlaps the left. Try the skirt on and mark the point where the right-hand edge lies over the left. Sew on the two hook-and-eye fastenings to fasten the skirt.

7 Pin and machine-stitch three rows of ribbon around the bottom of the skirt, using matching thread and a line of stitching along both edges of each ribbon. Start with the green ribbon, positioning it 5mm from the bottom edge of the skirt and folding the ends over to the inside. Space the ribbons 5mm apart and parallel to each other, with the red ribbon above the green one and the blue ribbon at the top.

In the same way, sew three rows of ribbon around the waistband, with the blue ribbon along the top edge, red in the middle and green below.

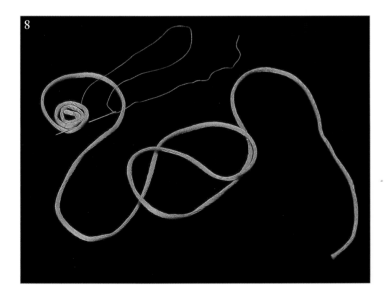

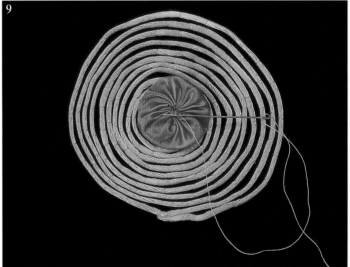

8 Mark the positions for your seven cord circles with pins, placing them at different heights. Start near the right-hand opening but make sure none of the circles will be under the wrapover. To couch the cords on, use a single matching thread. Start with a few stitches in the centre of the circle, then hand-sew into the end of the cord and over it a few times to secure it. Make a long stitch on the wrong side of the skirt and a small stitch over the cord, coiling the cord as you go.

9 Finish by tucking the end of the cord under the last coil and stitching through it.

Following the instructions on page 19 and using the matching circles of fabric, make a Suffolk puff to sew into the centre of each cord circle. Sew a cluster of three matching beads into the centre of each Suffolk puff.

Top with Box-pleat Neckline

*I love the fresh colour of this top and its simple scooped neckline is ideal
to decorate. I box-pleated both ribbons before sewing them around the
neckline, achieving an interesting effect by using the same technique
on two types of ribbon. Keeping everything the same colour makes the
different qualities of the organza and satin more obvious.*

You will need

Pale green top with a scooped neckline –
this will lose its elasticity once the ribbon
is sewn on, so you need to be able to put
it over your head without stretching it.

Mint-green satin ribbon 25mm wide – a
length three times the circumference of
the neckline plus 20cm

Pale green organza ribbon 20mm wide –
length as above

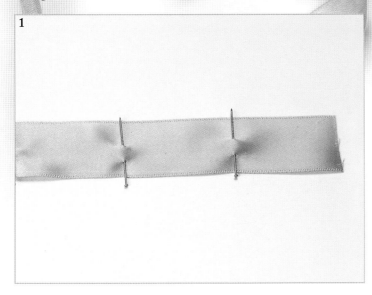

1 To box-pleat the satin ribbon, start at the right-hand end of the
ribbon and put a pin 4cm from the end. Then put another five
pins in the ribbon, one every 4cm.

2 Fold the ribbon to the right, so the first pin is in line with the
right-hand end, and pin this pleat in place. Now fold the ribbon
to the left at the second pin, bringing it into line with the third pin,
and pin in place.

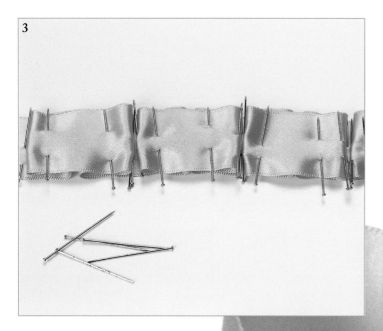

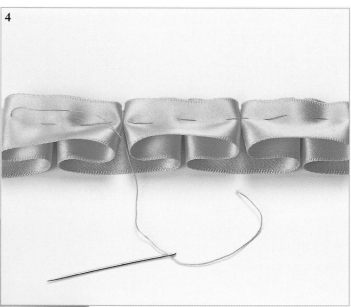

3 Continue pleating by folding the ribbon to the right at the fourth pin, bringing it into line with the third pin, and pin in place. Then fold the ribbon to the left at the fifth pin, bringing it into line with the sixth pin, and again pin in place. Remove the marker pins from this section.

4 Repeat this process until the box-pleated ribbon is long enough to go around the neckline of your top. Allow for the fact that the satin ribbon will be attached below the organza ribbon, so it will need to be slightly longer than the edge of the neckline itself. Cut the ribbon, leaving an extra 1cm.

Tack the pleats in place by sewing a line of running stitches just above the centre of the ribbon.

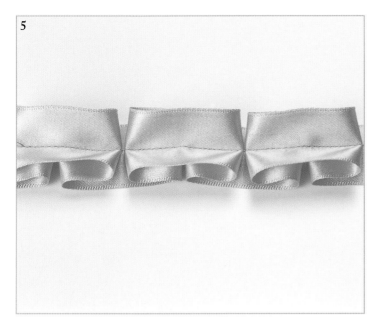

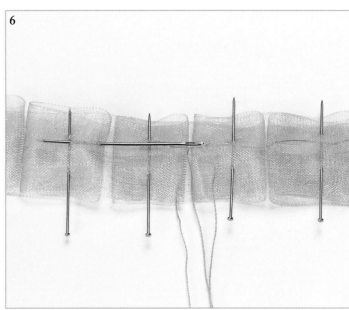

5 Machine-stitch along the centre of the pleated ribbon, leaving the long thread ends uncut. Remove the tacking.

6 Box-pleat the organza ribbon in exactly the same way.

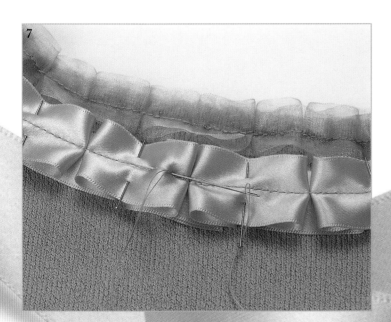

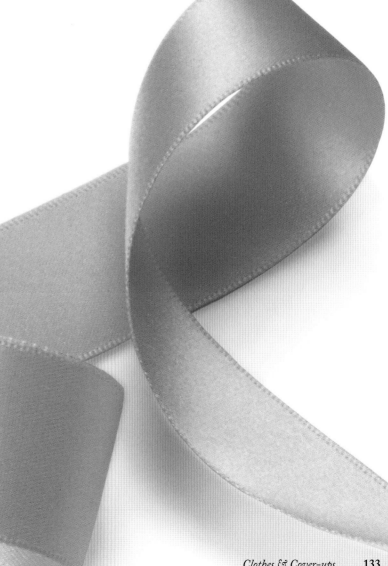

7 To attach the box-pleated ribbons to the top, start at the centre back of the neckline and pin the organza ribbon in place first around the edge of the neckline. Tuck the raw ends under the pleats where they meet. Hand-sew the pleated ribbon in place with running stitch, making tiny stitches on top of the ribbon and longer ones on the wrong side of the top. Use the ends of the machine threads to do this.

Sew the box-pleated satin ribbon on in the same way, positioning it just below the organza ribbon.

Cardigan with Cut-ribbon Work

The cut-ribbon work I have used for this project creates a wonderful textural effect and gives this fine-knit silk cardigan a three-dimensional quality, while the unusual colour combination creates a vintage feel. Once the ribbon is cut, you can curve it into all sorts of patterns, so experiment with different designs to suit your cardigan.

You will need

Taupe cardigan

Olive-green taffeta ribbon 24mm wide – 1m

Tobacco-green silk ribbon 24mm wide – 1m

Beige silk satin ribbon 14mm wide – 1m

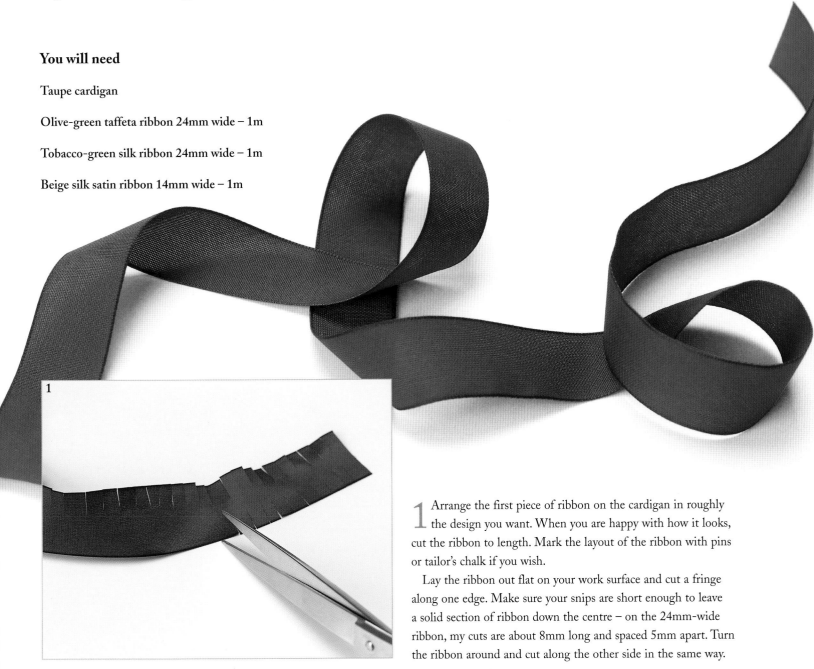

1 Arrange the first piece of ribbon on the cardigan in roughly the design you want. When you are happy with how it looks, cut the ribbon to length. Mark the layout of the ribbon with pins or tailor's chalk if you wish.

Lay the ribbon out flat on your work surface and cut a fringe along one edge. Make sure your snips are short enough to leave a solid section of ribbon down the centre – on the 24mm-wide ribbon, my cuts are about 8mm long and spaced 5mm apart. Turn the ribbon around and cut along the other side in the same way.

2 Arrange the cut ribbon on the cardigan in your chosen pattern and, starting at one end, tack it in place with running stitch using a single thread. Ease the ribbon into the shape of your design as you sew and be careful to keep the cardigan flat and smooth.

3 Machine-stitch the ribbon in place on the cardigan, sewing along the centre of the ribbon. Finish the machine-thread ends off by hand on the inside of the cardigan. Remove the tacking thread.

4 Continue to build up your design using the other ribbons and sewing them on in the same way.

Denim Jacket & Knickerbockers

Inspired by old-fashioned knickerbockers, here is a great way to reinvent a favourite pair of jeans and breathe new life into a denim jacket, making a smart boho-style two-piece. The two shades of blue lace are more subtle than white lace would be, and covering the buttons in blue velvet gives the jacket a more sophisticated look.

You will need

Denim jacket

Pair of jeans with a loose fit on the leg

Dark blue lace trim 80mm wide – a length twice the circumference of each cuff and each leg below the knee

Light blue lace trim 3cm wide – sufficient to stitch to your garments as you wish (I used 6m)

Blue velvet ribbon 7mm wide – sufficient to stitch to your jacket as you wish and for two drawstrings for the knickerbockers (I used 3m)

Self-cover buttons – sufficient for your jacket in a diameter to fit the buttonholes

Wide velvet ribbon to cover the buttons

Clear nail varnish

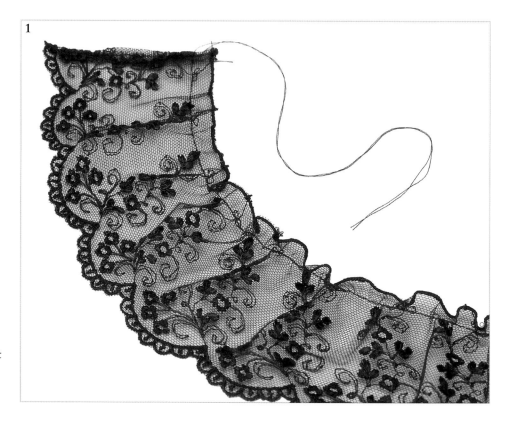

1 First remove all the buttons from the jacket. Then sew the dark blue lace to the cuffs. To do this, cut a length of lace twice the circumference of the cuff. Turn the ends under twice by 5mm and machine-stitch the hems down. Set the machine to a long stitch length and loosen the tension, then sew a line of gathering stitches 1cm down from the top edge of the lace, on the right side.

2 Pin both ends of the lace to the side seam of the cuff at the gathered edge, with the right side of the lace to the wrong side of the cuff. Pull the gathering thread – the bobbin thread, which will be on top – to gather up the lace. Once the lace fits around the hem of the cuff, secure the threads by winding them in a figure-of-eight around the two pins at each end. Spread the gathers out evenly and pin the lace in place.

3 Machine-stitch the lace onto the cuff from the right side and hand-sew the thread ends to secure. Repeat on the other cuff.

4 Trim the jacket with light blue lace – where you position this will depend on the style of your jacket. I attached some around the collar, pockets and bottom hem, but you can choose other seam lines to decorate as you wish. Work out how much lace you will need to trim your pocket, for example, and cut it to length with an extra 1cm hem allowance. Turn the ends of the lace under by 5mm and pin it in place, then machine-stitch the lace onto the jacket. When you need to sew around a corner, make small tucks to ease the lace into position. Use the long ends of the threads to hand-sew the hems down.

Machine-stitch some light blue lace around the cuffs, positioning it so that it overlaps the dark blue lace.

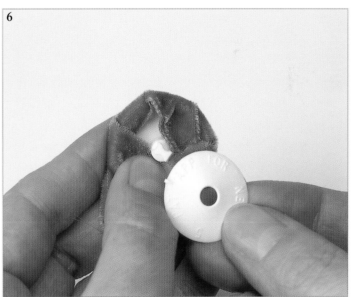

5 Decide where to attach strips of velvet ribbon. I put them across the pocket flap and around the cuff. Pin the ribbon into place, tucking the raw ends under, and machine-stitch with one line of stitching along the top edge. Hand-sew the thread ends to secure.

6 Cut a piece of velvet ribbon large enough to cover the front of your self-cover buttons. Follow the manufacturer's instructions to cover the buttons, then sew the buttons onto your jacket.

7 For the knickerbockers, the hem will form a casing through which to thread the drawstring ribbon. Cut your jeans off 12cm below the bottom of your kneecap. Unpick the bottom 6cm of the outside leg seam. Cut across one half of the seam allowance at the top so that the two halves can be opened out. Machine-stitch in place.

8 Press under a 1cm hem then a 2.5cm hem. Pin and machine-stitch in place, going back over the stitch line a little way at the beginning and end to secure it.

9 Decorate the hem of the knickerbockers with lace in the same way as for the cuffs. To do this, for each leg, cut a length of dark blue lace twice the circumference of the hem. Turn the ends of the lace under by 5mm and machine-stitch the hems down. Gather the lace and sew it around the bottom of the knickerbockers exactly as you did with the cuffs on the jacket (see steps 1–3).

Machine-stitch some light blue lace around the hem, overlapping the dark blue lace as before. Leave enough space in the hem to thread the velvet ribbon through.

For the drawstring, use a length of velvet ribbon long enough to fit through the hem plus 50cm to tie the bow. Secure a safety pin at one end of the ribbon and use this to feed the ribbon through the casing. Paint clear nail varnish on the raw ends of the ribbon to prevent them from fraying.

Sew two more covered buttons on the outside leg seam – just above the opening.

Repeat for the other leg.

Winter Coat with Quilted Ribbon

This coat is decorated with lengths of ribbon that have been machine-quilted and embroidered to give them a raised surface and textural detail. The folded and pointed ribbon ends finished with buttons were inspired by a coat design on a fashion illustration from the early 1900s. The buttons are kept simple so as not to distract from the ribbon detail.

You will need

Winter aubergine coat

Brown matt satin ribbon 50mm wide – sufficient to go around both sleeves and the bottom of the coat with a 10cm gap at the front on either side, plus 2cm for hems and 18cm for the buttons

Four self-cover buttons – 22mm diameter

Optional extra self-cover buttons if you decide to change the ones on the coat

Brown silk fabric – sufficient to cover all the buttons

Lightweight quilter's wadding 3.5cm wide – the same length as the brown satin ribbon

Muslin fabric 3.5cm wide – the same length as the wadding

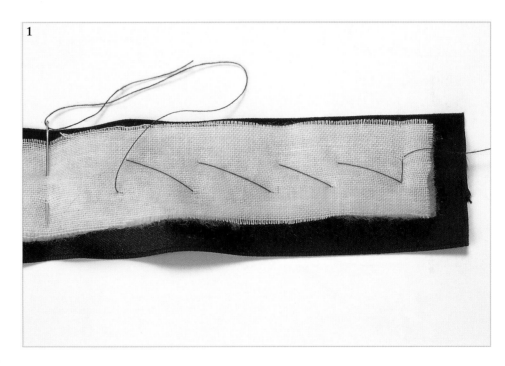

1 Cut sufficient brown satin ribbon to go around the hem of your coat, stopping 10cm from the front on both sides and adding an extra 2cm for the hems. Cut the wadding and muslin to the same length minus the extra 2cm.

Lay the ribbon right side down on your work surface and place the wadding on top, then place the muslin on top of the wadding. Keeping the layers flat, tack into place – start with a backstitch then make a 2cm-long diagonal stitch on the muslin, followed by a short horizontal stitch on the front of the ribbon.

2

2 Set up your sewing machine to quilt and embroider – you will need to attach the embroidery foot and lower the feed dog. Set the stitch to a medium length. Choose two coloured threads that will show up on the ribbon and tone in with your coat. Thread the machine with the first colour and then quilt and embroider a freestyle pattern along the centre of the ribbon. Keep the ribbon very flat by holding it firmly with both hands as you stitch.

3 Quilt and embroider along the ribbon in your second colour in the same way.

3

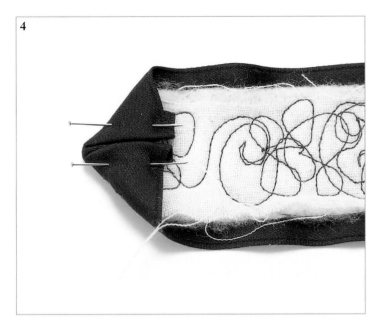

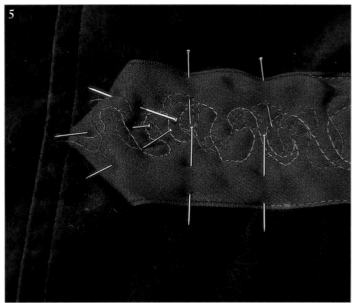

4 To make the pointed ends at the end of the quilted-ribbon band, fold the raw end of the ribbon in by 5mm, then fold the corners in to form a triangle shape and pin in place.

5 Pin the quilted ribbon band 9cm up from the bottom of the coat, starting and finishing 10cm in from each edge. Make sure the ribbon is straight and then machine-stitch it in place. If the lining of your coat is sewn in at the bottom, take care to keep the lining flat as you pin and sew. If it is loose, you don't need to stitch through it, so keep it out of the way as you sew.

6 Quilt and embroider the ribbon for the sleeves in the same way. You can make one length for both sleeves and cut it in half when it is finished. Leave these cut ends straight but make the other end of the bands pointed. Pin and machine-stitch the quilted-ribbon bands to the sleeves, positioning them 5cm up from the hem and lining up the straight edge of the band with the seam on the underside of the sleeve.

For the buttons, use a 4.5cm strip of matching brown satin ribbon to cover the four buttons, following the manufacturer's instructions. Sew a button onto the pointed end of the ribbon bands on the coat and sleeves.

I also changed the buttons on my coat and covered them in matching brown silk.

Strappy Black Evening Top

A simple black silk camisole has been transformed into a stunning party top by the addition of glamorous ribbons and trimmings. I loved the idea of these off-the-shoulder bows, inspired by a dress illustration from the 1890s. The black woven braid has a subtle sparkle, while the silver braid and beads add a sprinkling of glitter.

You will need

Black strappy top

Black velvet elastic 16mm wide – 50cm

Black sparkly braid 28mm wide – 1m

Glittery braid 2mm wide – 1m

Black beads – 5mm diameter

Black satin ribbon 48mm wide – 1.4m

Clear nail varnish

1 To make the off-the-shoulder straps, pin one end of the black velvet elastic to the bottom of the back strap, folding the end under on the wrong side of the strap. Try on your top, then bring the elastic across your upper arm and pin it at the same level on the front strap – you may need someone to help you. The elastic should fit snugly over your arm. Take the top off, then cut the elastic to the correct length, leaving sufficient to fold the end under on the wrong side of the front strap. Machine-stitch the elastic to the straps.

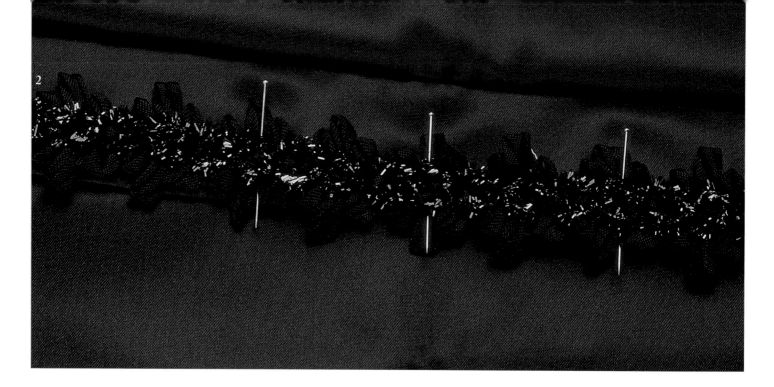

2 Where you decide to attach your braids will depend on the style of your top. Around the neckline and hemline are good places. My top has a feature tuck under the bustline that I decorated as well.

First pin the wide sparkly braid on, turning the raw ends under, and machine-stitch in place. Then pin and machine-stitch the narrow glittery braid on in the same way.

3 Sew beads onto the top wherever you like – I used mine to hide the ends of the glittery braid.

4 Cut two 70cm lengths of black satin ribbon and tie a bow with each, following the instructions on pages 14–15. Make sure the centre of the bow is neat and that the two loops are the same size.

5 Lay the bow down flat and trim the ends of the ribbon diagonally so that they are the same length, approximately 10cm. Paint the ends with clear nail varnish to prevent them from fraying.

6 To attach the bows to the shoulder straps, thread a needle with a single thread and, working at the back of the bow, make several stitches to secure the knot. Using the same thread, hand-sew the bow to the centre of the velvet elastic. Hold the underside of the bow loops in place with several small stitches approximately 2.5cm along on both sides of the central knot.

Circular Wrapover Skirt Diagram

(page 126)

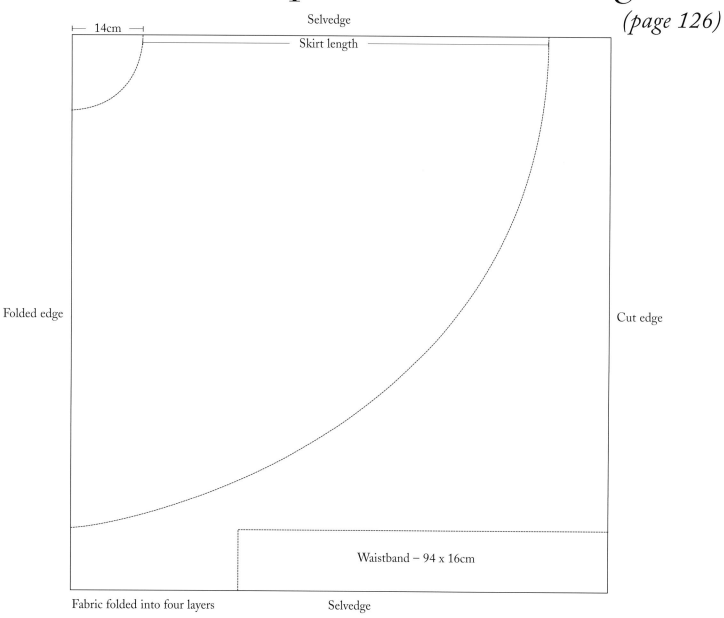

Selvedge

14cm

Skirt length

Folded edge

Cut edge

Waistband – 94 x 16cm

Fabric folded into four layers

Selvedge

Cutting out the skirt

Lay out the fabric on a large flat surface. Fold it in half, bringing the cut ends together. Then fold it in half again so it is four layers deep and almost square. Turn the folded fabric so that you have all the folded edges to your left and the cut edges to your right, with the selvedges at the top and bottom (as shown above).

Referring to the diagram above, mark out the skirt shape on your fabric using tailor's chalk or a fabric-marker pen. To do this, hold a tape measure at the top left corner and mark a point 14cm down the left-hand edge, then pivot the tape measure and mark another point 14cm along the top edge. Pivot the tape measure diagonally and mark

a third point 14cm from the corner. Join these points together in a curve, so that it measures 24cm – this is the waistline but not the finished waist size, as the skirt overlaps.

Measure 88cm down from the waistline. This will be the length of your skirt – if you change it, don't forget to allow 3cm for the seams. Using a tape measure as before, mark points 6cm apart, 88cm down from the waistline curve to form a second curve. Cut out the skirt.

To cut out the waistband, open out the remaining fabric and cut out a rectangle measuring 94 x 16cm with the selvedge along one side. Cut out a piece of iron-on interfacing measuring 94 x 8cm.

Emerald Beaded Bag Template

(page 92)

Enlarge on a photocopier by 200 per cent

Centre fold line

39cm

18cm

Clutch Bag
Template
(page 96)

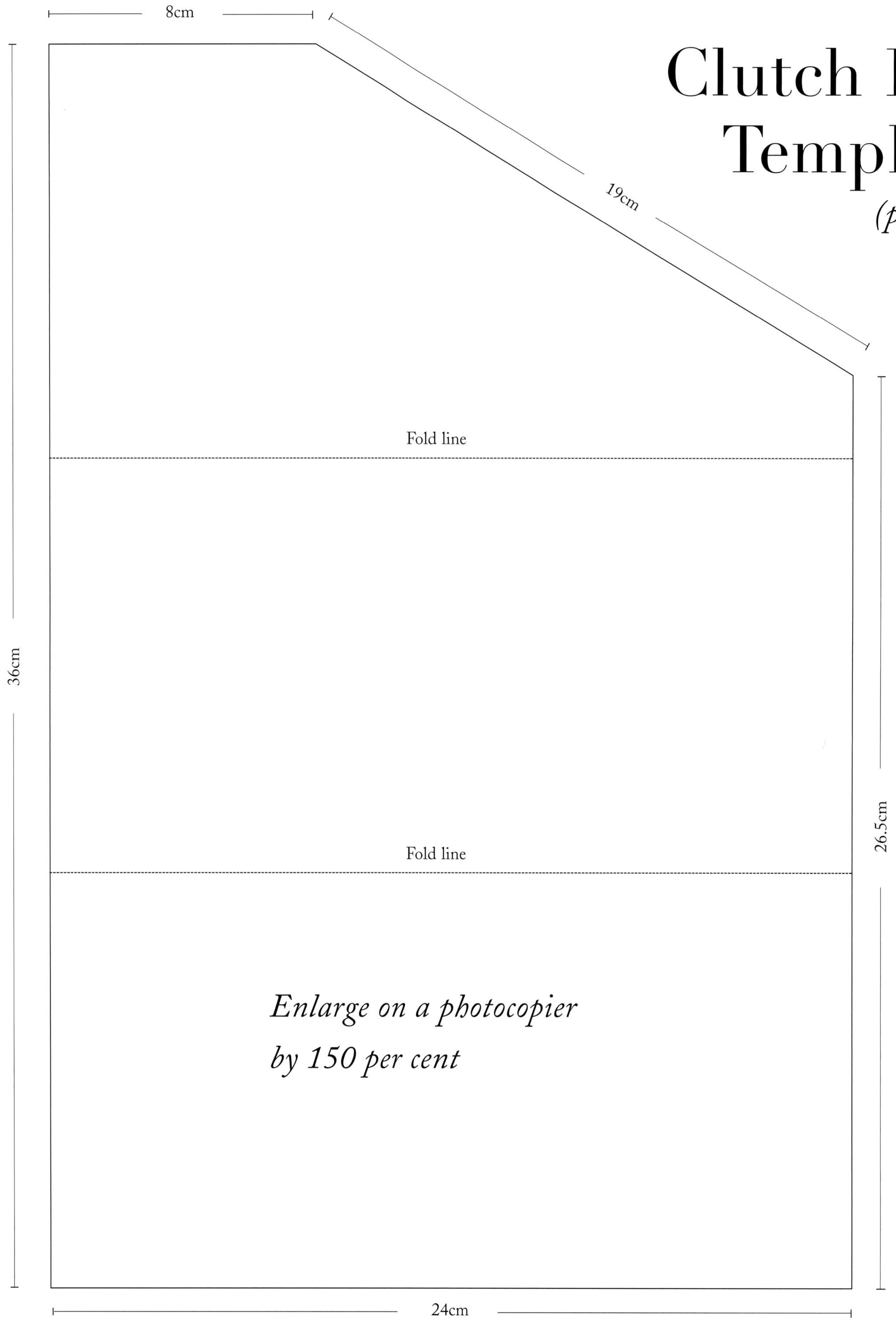

8cm

19cm

36cm

26.5cm

Fold line

Fold line

Enlarge on a photocopier
by 150 per cent

24cm

Tasselled Bag Template *(page 104)*

Enlarge on a photocopier by 200 per cent

30cm

26cm

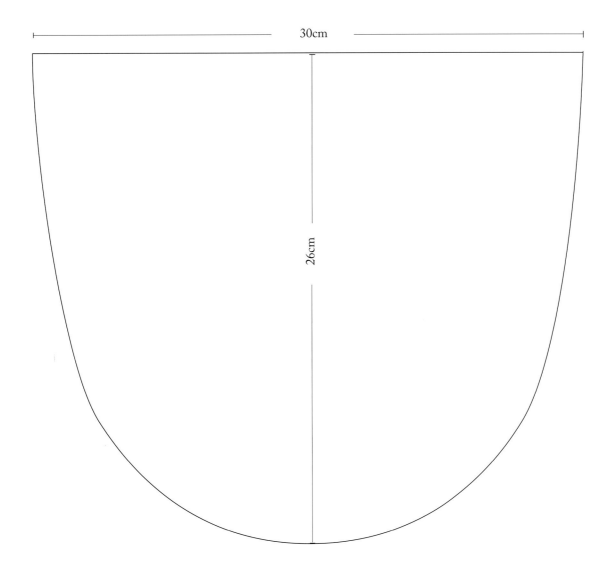

Address Book

RIBBONS, TRIMS, FABRIC & HABERDASHERY

Cath Kidston
51 Marylebone High Street,
London W1 5HW
Tel: 020 7935 6555
www.cathkidston.co.uk
*Vintage-style fabrics and some sewing accessories.
You can also shop online.*

The Cloth House
47 Berwick Street, London W1F 8SJ
Tel: 020 7437 5155
www.clothhouse.com
*Shop specializing in natural fabrics
and vintage trimmings.*

Coats Crafts
PO Box 22, Lingfield House, Lingfield Point,
McMullen Road, Darlington,
County Durham DL1 1YQ
For details of a local stockist,
call 01325 394 237
or email the consumer helpline
consumer.ccuk@coats.com
www.coatscrafts.co.uk
*Large supplier of needlecraft products, including
brands such as Sylko and Anchor threads.*

Fibrecrafts
Old Portsmouth Road, Peasmarsh, Guildford,
Surrey GU3 1LZ
Tel: 01483 565 800
www.fibrecrafts.com
*Equipment and materials such as dyes, fibres,
silk and cotton fabrics.*

John Lewis
Oxford Street, London W1A 1EX
Tel: 020 7629 7711
Customer services 0845 049 049
www.johnlewis.com
*Stores nationwide. Good haberdashery
department and dressmaking fabrics.*

Kleins
5 Noel Street, London W1F 8GD
Tel: 020 7437 6162
www.kleins.co.uk
Specialist haberdashery shop.

Liberty
Regent Street, London W1B 5AH
Tel: 020 7734 1234
www.liberty.co.uk
*Fabrics and haberdashery department selling
threads and useful accessories.*

Rainbow Silks
85 High Street, Great Missenden, Bucks
HP16 0AL
Tel: 01494 862 929
www.rainbowsilks.co.uk
*Creative embroidery products,
iron-on adhesive, shell buttons,
and so on. Mail-order service.*

Sew Essential Ltd
Burleigh House, 2 Box Street, Walsall,
West Midlands WS1 2JR
Tel: 01922 722 276
www.sewessential.co.uk
*Online sewing superstore selling all those
essential bits and pieces, from bag handles
to threads and ribbons.*

V V Rouleaux
54 Sloane Square, London SW1 8AX
Tel: 020 7730 3125
www.vvrouleaux.com
*The leading ribbons and trimmings brand.
If they haven't got it, no one has.
Mail order available.*

Wolfin Textiles Ltd
359 Uxbridge Road, Hatch End, Middlesex
HA5 4JN
Tel: 020 8428 9911
www.wolfintextiles.co.uk
*Large range of natural and bleached cotton and
linen fabrics.*

BEADS & BUTTONS

The Bead Shop
7 Market Street, Nottingham NG1 6HY
Tel: 0115 958 8899
www.mailorder-beads.co.uk
International online mail-order beads.

The Brighton Bead Shop
21 Sydney Street, Brighton, BN1 4EN
Tel: 01273 740 777
www.beadsunlimited.co.uk
Phone for the catalogue or order through the website.

The Button Queen
19 Marylebone Lane, London W1U 2NF
Tel: 020 7935 1505
www.thebuttonqueen.co.uk
A family-run shop specializing in antique and modern buttons.

INEXPENSIVE CLOTHING TO CUSTOMIZE

H&M
234 Regent Street, London W13 3BR
Tel: 020 7758 3990
www.hm.com

New Look
500–502 Oxford Street, London W1C 2HW
Tel: 020 7290 7860
www.newlook.co.uk

Primark
499–517 Oxford Street, London W1K 7DA
Tel: 020 7495 0420
www.primark.co.uk

VINTAGE

Portobello Road Market
Portobello Road/Westbourne Grove,
London W11
Tel: 020 7229 8354
www.portobelloroad.co.uk
Street market selling new and vintage clothes, jewellery and bric-a-brac – Saturdays only 5.30am–5pm.

eBay.co.uk / eBay.com
Web-based auction site for anything and everything – a good place to pick up bargains.

Index

Acknowledgements

I would like to thank Jacqui Small and Joanna Copestick for coming up with such a wonderful idea and for asking me to do it – it has been an inspiration.

Thank you also for putting together such an excellent team.
Sian – your photography is beautiful and a big 'thank you' to you and your family for the warm welcome and relaxed atmosphere at all our locations.
Barbara – thank you for organizing us all so that things ran so smoothly and for the fabulous design work.
Zia – your patience and attention to detail are quite incredible and, along with all your advice, very much appreciated – thank you.

I would like to thank Lucy and Ruvani for modelling my creations so stylishly.

Thank you also to the staff at V V Rouleaux Sloane Square.

Thank you to my friends and family, who have supported me throughout with such enthusiastic encouragement and looked after Sam and Nat while I've been stitching away.

Thanks to my mum, Jeanne, for inspiring me to sew in the first place and for donating her vintage white mohair scarf to be customized.

Special thanks to Rick, whose enduring love and support, as always, make all things possible.